Outsider

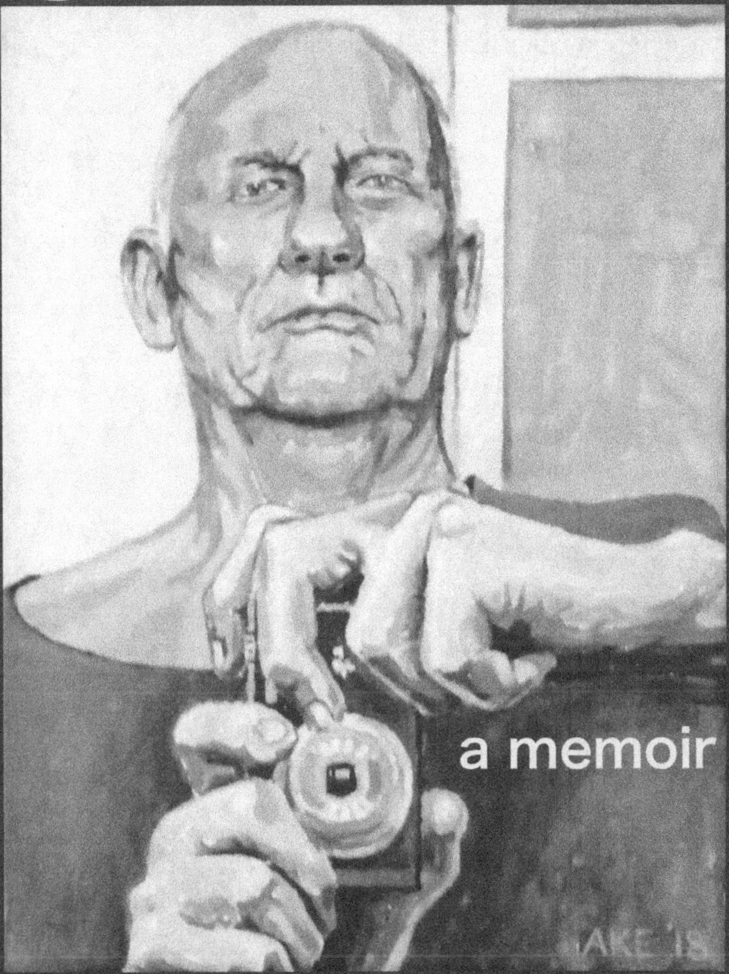

a memoir

Jeremy Akerman

Cover image: Jeremy Akerman self-portrait
Cover layout: Rebekah Wetmore

Editor: Andrew Wetmore

ISBN: 978-1-990187-31-5
First edition May, 2022

MOOSE HOUSE
PUBLICATIONS

2475 Perotte Road
Annapolis County, NS
B0S 1A0

moosehousepress.com
info@moosehousepress.com

We live and work in Mi'kma'ki, the ancestral and unceded territory of the Mi'kmaw people. This territory is covered by the "Treaties of Peace and Friendship" which Mi'kmaw and Wolastoqiyik (Maliseet) people first signed with the British Crown in 1725. The treaties did not deal with surrender of lands and resources but in fact recognized Mi'kmaq and Wolastoqiyik (Maliseet) title and established the rules for what was to be an ongoing relationship between nations. We are all Treaty people.

Also by Jeremy Akerman

What Have You Done for Me Lately?
First edition Lancelot Press, 1977
Revised edition Moose House Publications, 2022

Black Around the Eyes
First edition McClelland & Stewart, 1981
Second edition Moose House Publications, 2022

Foreword

John Leefe

Too few insiders have put pen to paper to recount stories of Nova Scotia's body politic. Graham Steele, by every measure the best minister in the short-lived Dexter administration, continues to be the most prolific. Ed Haliburton, a well-known member of the Stanfield and Smith administrations, wrote extensively on his political experiences at Province House. Jeremy Akerman offered up a brief and instructive book explaining provincial government aptly titled, *What Have You Done for Me Lately?* which I readily admit to using while teaching in the '70s. Otherwise, little has been written of the pithy side of politics.

Those who have served as MLAs measure their colleagues on both sides of the House, some more critically than others. In my years, 1978-1999, there was a certain collegiality that engendered many cross-party friendships which have endured long past life in elected office. There were members who were larger than life. Jerry Regan, John Buchanan, Rollie Thornhill and Akerman himself and his constant friend and supporter Paul MacEwan, among others, leap to mind. Most of us were essentially part of the furniture, there to do a job for the people who sent us and, if fortunate enough to be in cabinet, to have the opportunity to be something of a mover and a shaker.

Jeremy is the first and, I hope, not the last to offer a memoir not only of political life but of the circuitous route that took him and indeed most of us to Province House. I had the good fortune to hear Jeremy in debate. Erudite, focused, fiery, humorous, pithy, he kept the interest of all members. He was collegial with many from "the other sides", what one would call a House of Commons Man. In life after the Legislature, he became something of a political chameleon, but always within the context of some facet of government. I wouldn't say his talents went to waste, but they were never utilized to the full benefit of the agencies where he found shelter.

In addition to being an author, Jeremy was an enthusiastic thespian, a characteristic that clearly has stood him in good stead in life at Province House and on the hustings. Whether speaking, putting questions to ministers or in media scrums, he always performed well.

This memoir is something of a departure for Jeremy in that it is a pithy, sometimes punishing, analysis of the many who have crossed his path in life, occasionally offered with some degree of hyperbole which others might call literary licence. Personalities are laid bare, fools not suffered, friendships cherished, lost opportunities lamented. It is also transformative, with Jeremy's professed revelation that the NDP was metamorphosing from a working man's party to one lead by social workers, academics and lawyers.

This memoir is an important addition to the story of Nova Scotia's body politic. Rather than a tight chronological history, it almost verges from time to time into stream of consciousness, making it a different read than the scribblings of his predecessors.

Despite the vicissitudes of life, Jeremy has retained a real and vital interest in the political life of Nova Scotia and has cherished the collegiality of time past that offered friendships across party lines.

Most books about the province's politics are written from 30,000 feet. This one focuses on ground zero, which makes it a particularly important contribution to the genre.

John Leefe was Conservative MLA for Queens from 1978 to 1999, and Mayor of the Municipality of Queens from 2000-2012. He is Honorary Colonel of the West Nova Scotia Regiment, and the recipient of the Canada 125, Queen's Golden Jubilee and Queen's Diamond Jubilee decorations. In 2002 he was granted the degree of Doctor of Civil Law by the University of King's College. In 2010 he received the Ambassador Award for support of the tourism industry.

Remembrance, not history

This is a memoir, not a history. The contents of this book come from my mind, not from dusty tomes, public records or Wikipedia. You will not find learned footnotes or densely-researched passages, but I hope it may the more readable for that.

I have been greatly blessed to have an excellent memory, which some have described as "photographic". Faces, places and entire conversations from 75 years ago are still clear to me. However, it is inevitable that I will not always achieve 100% accuracy, or without exception place events in their correct time slot. This is because some events had a sameness to them (such as federal-provincial conferences and sessions of the Legislature), so it is not always possible to be precise that an event or conversation took place at conference A or conference C, or at a Tuesday sitting or a Thursday session.

As my friend Graham Steele points out in his excellent book *Nova Scotia Politics 1945-2020*, memoirs can sometimes be dangerously misleading because the memorialists often slant their accounts to show themselves as heroes and their adversaries as villains. Since many of the people of whom I write have passed on, they cannot refute or amend what I say about them, so you will just have to take my word that events happened in the way I describe. Even should you disbelieve what I say, I still hope you will find it entertaining.

When he knew I would finally be writing this book, Graham gave me one piece of advice: "Be candid. Tell it the way it really happened."

I have followed that advice in the full knowledge that it may get me into some trouble and/or make me some new enemies, but Orwell was right. So was Phillip Pulman when he said, "No one has the right to live without being shocked. No one has the right to spend their life without being offended."

I am extremely grateful to Ron Fisher and Arthur Donahoe for having read the manuscript and making comments and suggestions. Appreciative thanks are due to Graham Steele for repeatedly urging me to write this book. I am also greatly indebted to John Leefe for his foreword and to my wonderful wife, Carol Anne, for her unending support and encouragement.

JBA, 2021

To those who have tried, but have never quite made it

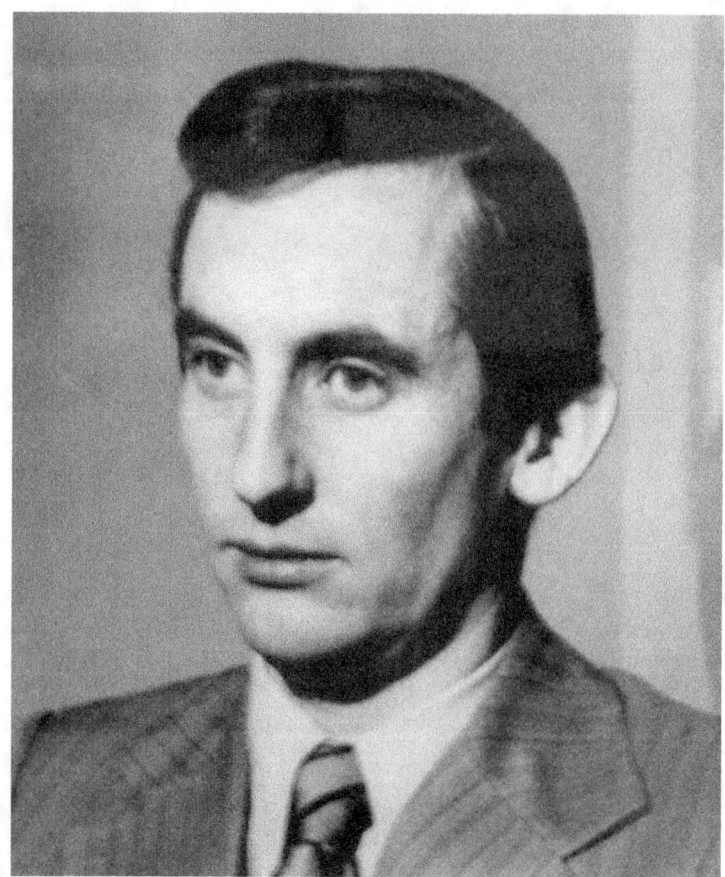

Portrait of the author as a young politician

Contents

Jeremy Akerman

1: Family

Akerman is not nearly as rare a family name as my family would like to think, but it is by no means common. For example, the 1851 census reveals there were about 500 Akerman families in England that year, and there were only around 400 in 1881. Some say the name derives from a man who owned a single acre; others say it originates in Jutland or Friesland in northeastern Europe.

The earliest reference to the Akermans I have seen is from the early medieval period, when people of that name held land in fee at Eyford from the Norman baron to whom the King had granted the lands in that area of the Cotswolds. Eyford is a lovely place about a mile north of Upper Slaughter.

Subsequent to the medieval reference, in 1601 an Elizabeth Akerman is recorded as having been baptized in Naunton (about six miles southwest of Longborough). A little later there was a Henry Akerman, "a poor servant of this parish", who died in Upper Slaughter in 1615. We can probably never know if we are connected to these Akermans, but it is does not seem entirely impossible that at least some of the Cotswold Akermans are descended, in one way or another, from the Akermans who were at Eyford not long after The Norman Conquest.

The earliest provable ancestor is my great, great, great grandfather William (born 1785), who is recorded as having been in Longborough in 1841. Almost all successive Akermans were agricultural labourers, carters and horse grooms.

My father, Bernard, was born in Warwick in 1907, his father, Frank, having been a carter and his mother, Jinnie (Mary Ann), a household maid. Both were from the Midlands around Warwick. My mother's mother, Kizzie (Elizabeth), hailed from Kent in the southeast of England, while her father, Ernest, came from farming stock in Yorkshire in the northeast.

Dad's parents were poor, but he was able to "get ahead" by winning a scholarship to the posh Warwick School. Thereafter, he was employed in industry, either in sales and/or managerial capacities.

Mother had a sister, Nancy, who died in her teens, and a brother, Jack, whose thunderous snoring shook the entire house whenever he visited us. Dad had a sister, Myra, and brothers Maurice and Albert. Aunt Myra was a friendly woman whose life seemed devoted to her daughter, Valerie, and to her husband, Wilson, who was continually troubled with a "bad leg" (I never knew the cause of this affliction). Uncle Albert was a jocular, very pleasant man whom I greatly liked, but saw very seldom.

Dad's other brother (known to his nephews as "Mad Maurice") was our favourite relative as he was generous with his money, was always larking around, and gave us many amusing anecdotes and quotes which we repeat to this day. Single all his life, he lived with Grandmother Jinny until she died at 101. Maurice spoke at a rapid pace, had a weird, wheezing laugh and was a devotee of the Wild West, in particular the books of Zane Grey. He had served in Burma during WWII and his many eccentricities were attributed to his sufferings in the jungle and/or at the hands of the Japanese.

There is a remarkable fact about Maurice which few know: He worked on the line at the Lockheed aircraft factory and at the end of his shift, he would cycle into Leamington Spa to the Conservative Club, where he would preside over meetings of Prime Minister Anthony Eden's constituency association. He was a stereotypical working class Tory who adored Mrs. Thatcher, describing her as "a wonderful woman", and showed little acceptance of what today would be called "diversity". His racial tolerance diminished even further as he got older, and in his declining years often divested himself of startling characterizations. Once, he stood in the rain in our yard shaking his fist at the sky, shouting, "This is not England, it's Wogland!"

My brother Michael (who died in 2021) was born in 1938, I in

1942 and Andrew ten years after me. There was another brother who lived for only a few days about whom discussion was discouraged. My recollection is that his name was to have been Roger, but Andrew says it would have been Simon.

Mike and his wife Pat had three boys (one adopted) while Andrew and Amanda had a boy and a girl. My brothers had/have a number of grandchildren (seven, I believe), which I greatly envy as I can never have that joy.

During my early years in the political arena, from time to time I visited Ed Mackinnon of Coady Street in Sydney, Cape Breton. While there, I had noticed the graduation photograph of a stunning black-haired young woman who, he told me, was Joan, one of his three daughters.

After I had been defeated in the 1968 federal election, I went to Ontario to try to find some means of support. Having found no work, and having outstayed my welcome at several friends' houses, I was desperate. I was living out of my car in the woods in the Ottawa Valley, washing in streams and eating dry bread.

Then I remembered the photograph of Joan MacKinnon, and recalled that her father had told me she was attending Carleton University, so I drove into the city (my car had just enough gas to get there), went to a phone booth and, with what little money I had left, called Ed in Sydney. I lied, telling him I was fit and well, and said I just happened to be in the City, seemed to recall his daughter was living there, and if he would give me the address I would drop in to say hello.

I drove to the address on Besserer Street, parked and waited. And waited.

After some hours, I saw a woman who looked like Joan walking down the street, so I hopped out and introduced myself. Inside, I came clean about my predicament and asked if I could stay for a while. She agreed.

Several months later we were married in St. Patrick's Cathedral.

My ten years with Joan were filled with uncertainty, poverty and stress, although we had a good marriage until the demands of political life turned me into an irascible stranger. Years later, I asked Joan to forgive me for having been a lousy husband and she was kind enough to attribute all my errors and shortcomings to my having been too young. In 1974, in the midst of a provincial election, our son Gareth was born, curiously within a short time of the births of Gerald and Carole Regan's daughter Laura (now a fine Hollywood actress), and John and Mavis Buchanan's daughter Natasha.

Joan and I separated in 1978 and were divorced two years later. She was/is a very good woman, lively and intelligent, although stubborn and sometimes given to supernatural notions. After the naturally difficult divorce period, we became better friends than we had been when we were married, and I got along very well with her second husband, Fred, and their son, Michael.

It is inexpressibly sad that, at the time of writing, such a once lively and dynamic woman is suffering from dementia, having to be prevented from aimlessly wandering into the streets of Toronto. Also at the time of writing, I am still in touch with Joan's amazing, tough, and funny younger sister, Barbara, of whom my wife and I are inordinately fond. It is a very long time since I have seen any of her other siblings.

Gareth was a passionate naturalist and environmentalist, and when he was 33 accepted a post as a park ranger at the Black Hills National Forest in South Dakota. He planned to drive there from Florida, where, from the air, he had been tracking and recording migratory birds in the region of Lake Okeechobee.

The day before his planned departure for the Black Hills, he and two colleagues from the University of North Florida went up for one last survey. It seems the Cessna was overloaded, stalled, went into a tail spin, and crashed near Indiantown, a small community not far from Palm Beach. All three naturalists, together with the pilot, were killed, and in such a manner that none of the bodies was physically identifiable.

I often wonder what those ten seconds would have been like for Gareth when he knew he was plunging to his death.

He was a charming, entrancing child, and later the very best of all my friends. His living with his mother had meant that she had to handle discipline and tell him what he could and could not do, which luckily allowed me to be his buddy. Once, when he was over for supper, a friend called him. I could hear only one side of the conservation, but it filled me with delight: "I'm hanging with the J-Dog," Gareth said. "No, no problem, I'm staying. He's cool."

I could tell many anecdotes of my tall, lovely, shaggy son, but perhaps they belong to another book. Suffice it to say that on March 13, 2008, the light went out of my life until, some nine years later, my wonderful wife, Caroll Anne brought it back in.

Caroll Anne is from Birch Grove, Cape Breton, and we first met during the 1974 provincial election, and later spent some time together during her father Frank Boone's bid to win the Cape Breton West constituency in a by-election in 1976, when Attorney General Allan Sullivan resigned to become a judge. Subsequently, Caroll Anne moved to Halifax to work in the New Democratic Party (NDP) caucus office.

Our brief association at that time was blighted by circumstances, not least of which were the lies of others, but that will be of no interest to readers today. What may be of interest is that some 37 years later we found each other again via Facebook!

One day in 2017, I logged in and happened to see the name of her sister, Dayle, and through her I re-established contact with Caroll Anne. Our reunion was in the Halifax Public Gardens on a lovely sunny day.

We were married on July 4, 2018 by our very good friend, Supreme Court Justice Peter Bryson.

2: Beginnings

It was 14°C and sunny on the morning of May 28,1942 in Alvechurch, Worcestershire. Although the Luftwaffe had been heavily bombing the area regularly since 1940, they did not make a visit during this night, so the roar of Heinkels, Dorniers and Junkers did not drown out the cries of a newborn baby.

He was a lusty little fellow, I am told, and soon moved from the nursing home near the village square into a small semi-detached house further up the Birmingham Road. It was one of a dozen such houses on a service lane which looped from and back to the main road. I lived there until I was six, and it is of this place that my earliest memories shine as bright and sharp as if they happened last week.

Our neighbours on one side were the Stillwells. They had a daughter, Melanie, whom I met again by accident many years later. My mother said the Stillwells were "nice people". On the other side were the Coxes, whom my father described as "dreadful people". They had, in my mother's words, a "dirty little girl" called Madeline who peed in the garden and showed her private parts to anyone who cared to look.

My very earliest memory is of seeing the slotted masks on the headlights of my father's Austin 12, and hearing him explain that they directed light to the ground so as not to attract German bombers.

About the same time, I heard him say that his boss, Lord Austin, regularly patrolled the Austin factory's parking lot at nearby Long-bridge to see if any employees were driving his competitors' cars. If any were found, the owners were summarily told to "collect their cards" and go work for the other car maker.

When I was about two and a half, I recall my mother taking me on the bus to Birmingham, a huge city about 12 miles away. It was pitch black when we left, only the masked headlights of other vehicles occasionally punctuating the darkness.

At New Street station was a large, open, cobblestone area filled with horse-drawn wagons sporting various advertisements on their canvas sides. The one I liked best was for Digger Tobacco, which showed a ginger-bearded man wearing a cowboy hat and a red bandana, and smoking a bent pipe. Years later, I smoked Digger: It was almost black, had a wonderful aroma but burned the tongue ferociously.

On my brother Michael's ninth birthday, there was to be a party at our house at which sandwiches and hard to find cake were to be served. This would be a rare treat, as any kind of non- essential was hard to come by because food rationing was in full force; to make a cake required depriving ourselves for a week of butter and sugar and cutting back on flour.

Mike stood at the front door, and when the other kids arrived carrying their gifts, he snatched them out of their arms and tore back into the house. Showing the malicious side she always had in reserve, my mother cancelled the party and gave all the presents back. Poor Mike. He cried, and I cried too.

One day some little pals and I went down to the main Birmingham Road and threw gravel at passing vehicles. I have no idea why we did it, but we soon wished we hadn't.

A man braked his car, quickly hopped out and chased us up the lane. I ran round the house, in through the back and upstairs, where I peeped through the curtains.

The man knocked on the door and remonstrated with my mother. When he had gone, she gave me a stern lecture on how I could have killed people and sent me to bed without any lunch or supper.

At the end of the service lane, and just before it joined the main road, was a coppice of small trees and bushes where I sometime would hide if I was nursing a grievance. One day I crawled in and, to my delight and surprise, saw bright red cotton thread strung from branch to branch of the undergrowth. I followed it to the end, where, resting on the moss, was a shining sixpence! Day after day, I returned, but whilst the thread remained for quite some time, never again did this enchanted wonderland yield money. In any event, my mother took the sixpence, saying I was far too young to have any use for it.

Behind our row of houses was a large field in which the farmer grew potatoes and mangolds, a large root vegetable related to what we in Canada call turnips. I remember wandering into and around this field, being fascinated by large blocks of a bright blue substance which the cows eagerly licked. I later learned this was copper sulphate.

At first, those who worked picking the crop were members of the Women's Land Army, strapping young women all dressed alike, Wellington boots planted between the furrows and bums in air. Then they were replaced by Italian prisoners of war, men we thought of as dangerous, but who worked industriously and sang beautiful songs as they worked.

~

Early on weekday mornings, Dad drove my brother and me into Birmingham, where we attended a two-building school on Priory Road in the Edgbaston district. One building—for big kids like Mike, aged nine—was called Greenmore College, while the other—for little kids like me, aged five—boasted the name Farnborough House.

My class, of about forty children, was presided over by Mrs. Horseman, whose appearance did not belie her name. A younger, and much nicer looking lady, Miss Hollaway, was called upon from time to time to play patriotic tunes on the piano to which we were expected to sing. Every morning began with God Save the King, followed by The Twenty-third Psalm or All People That on Earth Do Dwell.

Few of my fellow pupils interested me, but I vividly recall two or three. One was my best friend, Maurice Cohen, a rumpled boy with unruly hair who resembled a worn-out teddy bear. Another was Margaret Onions, who insisted her surname was pronounced "Owneyeons". One most unfortunate little girl, who stammered and whimpered when called upon to speak, bore the unforgettable name of Cynthia Tit.

The last event I can remember taking place on our little lane was someone's idea of replicating the Olympic Games that took place in London in the summer of 1948. We kids were assigned countries (I was Belgium), and instructed to compete in egg and spoon, three legged, and sack races for tiny cans painted gold, silver and bronze. I hated this nonsense, as indeed I have hated all kinds of physical competition ever since. I particularly hated the local teacher having, stupidly, nailed a quantity of old rubber tire on to the end of an axe handle, which he lighted and pranced around, babbling about "the eternal flame". This contraption gave off billows of thick, evil-smelling black smoke which made my eyes water and caused me to cough helplessly. I have never been a fan of, or even been interested in, the Olympic Games since that time.

Shortly after the great Olympics and the burning tire, we learned that Dad had got a new job, as a buyer with the Girling Brake factory at Cwmbran in South Wales. What then seemed to me like an enormous brown van drew up outside and a gang of men loaded it with our belongings. I confess I have forgotten the name of the moving company, but I felt the company would probably lose or destroy our furniture because I had heard (and believed) that Pickford's big blue vans were the best.

I asked Dad why we couldn't have Pickford's and he muttered, "Too dear, too expensive." I was to hear him say that hundreds of times over the ensuing years.

In any event, away went the van and we followed in the Austin 12. Our destination, the little village of Castleton in Monmouthshire, was about 100 miles away to the southwest. Today, you could get there in an hour and a half. On the narrow, winding roads of 1948 it took nearly all day.

3: Croeso y Gymru

At that time it is doubtful that we passed a sign saying "Welcome to Wales" in Welsh near Little Doward on the A40, as pride in and consciousness of Welsh identity and culture were then relatively dormant in the south of the principality. Later such signs appeared all along the border with England, and within Wales all road signs became bilingual. For decades, they have been an uplifting sight to me, and whenever I see "Croeso y Gymru" my heart beats a little faster.

I shall not burden the reader with a list of the beauties of Wales, but will only say that if you have not been there, you have missed something very special indeed.

We arrived at Castleton in the early evening. The village of some fifty houses clustered around a junction of the main Cardiff-Newport road and a secondary road to Marshfield, a hamlet a few miles to the south. Our new house, called *Holmbank*, was some way down the secondary road on the right hand side. It was half of a fake Tudor duplex with a garden, a very large, unruly holly hedge, and an enormous oak tree in front. While the van men lugged the furniture into the house, I went exploring.

By the side of the house was a large wooden garage which contained a workbench, a large vise and some tools, and a row of huge metal bins which we later used to store grain for our chickens and which attracted dozens of huge rats. There were hooks on the wooden beams where I would hang my bicycle and a number of sacks filled with large nuts and bolts.

Behind the garage was a small concrete yard and a greenhouse in which Dad would grow tomatoes—whose delicious sweetness and wonderful aroma I can taste and smell to this day. When old people say we don't have tomatoes like they did back in the day, they are telling the truth!

Beside the greenhouse was a lawn, and beyond that a large, long garden in which there were numerous gooseberry and blackcurrant bushes, an evil-smelling cess pit covered with flag stones, and, at the top, a large wooden building divided into two sections. What purpose this shack had served was unclear to me, but mother called it "the potting shed", and later we kept pigs and then chickens in it.

Beyond the potting shed was an orchard of about eight apple trees, including a Russet which produced deliciously sweet fruit and a huge Bramley from the top of which I could see the roofs of the village, the sea and the islands of Flatholm and Steepholm in the Bristol Channel.

Beside the orchard was our very own private wood (which my mother insisted on calling "the spinney") consisting of some two dozen trees of different kinds and sizes. Behind the spinney was an immense grassy field containing a pond, huge horse chestnut trees and roaming cattle, some of them with horns. To a little kid of six this was absolute heaven!

I discovered that our property was wedged between two majors. On one side, the elderly and stately Major Williams lived with his wildly eccentric maid, Daisy, and an old white horse, Bill, who poked his head over the fence to be scratched and fed. On the other side lived Major James Smart, his wife Dorothy, daughter Gillian and son Francis, who went by the sobriquet "Boysie". Major Smart was stiff, voluble, and what in Cape Breton would be called "big feeling". He was an authority on everything and owned a .303 rifle which he took out and brandished from time to time.

Shortly after moving in, my parents decided that the house needed some sprucing up. So, on the recommendation of Henry Smith, landlord of The Angel pub, they hired a painter and decorator called Harold Bateman, whose family lived up road as tenants of District Nurse Cox (whom we kids called "Stumpy").

Mr. Bateman spent several weeks on the job, using on the walls of the outside toilet and conservatory a plaster-like product called Snowcem which I am told is still made today, is completely natural and contains no man-made plastics, polymers or solvents. I mention this only because its aroma was unique, and if I close my eyes I can still smell it 73 years on. It is indescribable, but is redolent of cleanliness and good health.

Much to Dad's disgust, Mr. Bateman insisted on being paid in cash. "Crafty blighter," Dad snorted, "trying to cheat the income tax. I pay mine, why shouldn't he pay his?"

"Pay him by cheque next time, Bernard," My mother said, but Dad just shrugged. He was never one for confrontation.

Mr. Bateman used to go home to tea (as the Welsh called the evening meal) around 5 pm, but occasionally delayed his departure if he were in the middle of a painting task which had to be completed so it could be dry by the next morning. On one such occasion there was a loud knocking on the front door and when my mother opened it, a small boy stood before her, plaintively whining:

"I want my tea."

"I don't have your tea," said Mum, "who are you?'

"I want my tea," wailed the child.

This went on for some minutes before Mr. Bateman rushed downstairs and announced that the child was his son, David. This was my introduction to the closest male friend I ever had and who was to be my inseparable companion for years to come.

It would be boring for the reader to recount the many adventures and escapades David (known as "Dai") Bateman and I experienced together over a 12-year period, but we roamed the fields, woods, and rivers; fished, stole apples, crawled through the undergrowth, climbed trees, vaulted gates; played pranks on old ladies, scared cattle and sheep, and annoyed farmers. One farmer I shall return to in a subsequent chapter.

Wherever we went, Dai and I imagined we were cowboys, bandits, US cavalry, WWII soldiers (the war had ended only a few years earlier), Knights of the Round Table, and various heroic or notorious figures. We even played *Richard III*, having seen Olivier's marvellous performance on screen, In every case, Dai would suggest the game and in the same breath assign to himself the junior role. "Let's play Robin Hood, I'm Little John". "Let's play Jesse James. I'm Frank".

He was younger than I and maybe not as intellectually sharp, but in most ways he was the superior of the two. Certainly, he was stronger, was infinitely better at sports, could fight (which I could not) when the need arose, and, when I got into scraps with other kids, Dai would step between us and make them back off.

Sometimes Russell Waters, another great friend with whom I am still in touch, would join us. Russ lived in the lodge or gate-house of the local manor, and later just up the road from us. He was a good and loyal friend, but I fear we did not always treat him as he deserved, and Dai sometimes mercilessly teased him. In a torrent of juvenile invective, Dai used to call him, "Russell John George dribbley gawky goony hooly gooly baldy baby."

Dai is no longer with us, but I offer Russell my unreserved apologies for any hurtful indignity we may have inflicted on him.

Other boys we hung out with in those years included Richard Furzee, who visited from Kettering on holidays; Dyfyd Thomas, the Baptist minister's son,;Clive Lewis, who called himself Mr. Horsey; Gareth Jones, the Anglican minister's boy; Graham Ballanger, whom Dai almost strangled on one occasion; Paul Waters; Roger Langsdowne, who was never shy about showing off his immense appendage; Vincent Rodway, who broke my brand new cricket bat; and other nefarious characters.

Collectively, we were responsible for a number of minor crimes and misdemeanours. Most of these would have been Breaking and Entering into abandoned War Department buildings which dotted the countryside and had been used for everything from barracks to the manufacture of munitions.

Usually, they were littered with equipment, sometimes clothing, tools, bales of wire and occasionally bullets, one of which was a huge .45. Later, we fixed this in the vise in Dad's garage and fired it by hammering a nail into its cap. It made a neat hole in the side of the garage and the noise was enough to awaken the dead. Also, I burned my hand and had to lie to my mother that I had sustained the injury while putting coal on the fire.

Another escapade in which the garage featured prominently was the skinning and alleged curing of a snake. Dai and I had seen it swimming in the Black Pond (so deep, it was said to have once totally enveloped a horse and cart) and had casually hurled sticks at it. To our surprise the poor beast floated to the surface.

I shall pass over the disgusting details of cutting, eviscerating and disembowelling it, and the rubbing it with salt and hanging it up from the garage rafters to cure and become usable as a belt. We left it there for months but, alas, its stench was as rank when we finally threw it away as it had been at the beginning.

~

It was during my years with Dai that I first really became aware of girls as something more than kids who were slightly different. Looking back, it strikes me that in our two villages we had more than our fair share of girls who were both nice and good looking, and only a few who were nasty or ugly.

In Marshfield, Regina Pretty, Denise Seabrook and Thelma David were lovely girls in every sense. Thelma was also a friend with whom I had actual interesting conversations. Her brother, Glyn, had a beautiful Raleigh racing bike with dropped handlebars which I mightily coveted. Thelma hooked up with one of my school mates, Graham Sully, whom I considered very lucky indeed, but I don't know if their relationship lasted into adulthood.

In Castleton, there were the Jones sisters, Carol and Brenda. Brenda was not only gorgeous but the nicest person you could wish to meet. On the other hand, Carol was large, loud, brash and would pitch a tiny pup tent in a field and invite boys in to feel her exposed breasts. The only time I crawled into the tent, there were already four boys inside, so I was unable to get anywhere near the objects of worship.

Hillary James was considered a rare beauty because she had a slightly Asiatic look, which she clearly inherited from her mother, but which her sister Leslie lacked. Her father was a physician who inoculated me against tuberculosis, a process he called a BCG. This was necessary due to my being a "contact" because my maternal grandmother, who lived with us, had once contracted the disease.

Elizabeth Crisp was a handsome and friendly girl, but was six feet tall and towered intimidatingly over us. Dai was in love with a lovely, raven-haired girl called Andrea Vitalis, who lived at the waterworks on the Michaelstone road not far from the village. His affection was unrequited. Norma Bergstrom had shiny long hair, was tall and very good looking, but mysterious and withdrawn. She seldom spoke, kept herself to herself and lived in a forbidding, creepy house at the end of a winding dirt lane behind the bakery.

But it was Valerie Knight who had most of us in thrall. She was spectacular in every physical respect (none of us got to know anything of her character) and had a host of admirers who would anonymously send her boxes of chocolates on Valentine's Day. I know this because I used to deliver evening newspapers for her father, Clive, and, when I went to collect them one night, saw these offerings stacked on their sideboard. I wonder Valerie retained her classic figure in view of the calories she must have consumed.

At the height of my infatuation, I used to go out after dark and stand in the bus shelter across from her house in hope that she might—for any reason—come out, see me and cross the road for a chat and who knows what else. She never did.

4: George and the farm

When we were about ten, Dai and I were gambolling across the fields when we saw a farmer ploughing, an activity I later came to adore and at which I became expert. When he got to our side of the field he stopped, turned off the tractor and sternly demanded to know what we were doing. Not knowing quite how to respond, I stammered that we came to see if there were any jobs we could do for him.

He sniffed, wiped his face with his cap (which he always wore backwards) and said, "If you were big enough you could keep the flies off the engine. But come back in the spring and I'll take you on for two and six an hour."

We eagerly accepted. If he was as good as his word, it would mean we would earn about $15 a day in 2021 money, a fortune to boys who were getting only $5 a week "pocket money" (allowance) from our parents.

This was the beginning of a rewarding, lucrative and character-building relationship, and of some of the happiest times of my life.

The farmer was George Clease, who owned Lower House Farm in Coedkernew, a small community about a mile from Castleton. You could reach it by taking the main road to Newport and then going right down a long, winding lane that ended in the farmyard. Dai and I could get there in 15 minutes by haring across the fields, something we did for years, every day on school holidays and every weekend summer and winter.

When we returned in the spring, George put us to work, and hard work it was, too. So laborious was it that at the end of the day we were so stiff and tired we swore we would not come back. But we did, time and again, until I was 18.

The tasks were many and varied, including making hay, planting and picking potatoes, cutting cabbage, collecting eggs, fertilizing the fields, muck spreading, ploughing, feeding the animals, bringing the cows up from the low pastures and milking them, and taking produce to the weekly market in Newport.

After a while, Russell joined us at the farm, although George was skeptical, saying with apparent, but not actual, profundity, "One boy is a boy. Two boys are half a boy. Three boys are no boys at all".

George had an annoying habit of assigning a task, doing it himself for three seconds to demonstrate how "easy" it was, disappearing for a while, then returning to demand why it was not completed. "It's only a five minute job," he would snort. "Come on, put your backs into it!"

We noticed that George himself undertook most of the less onerous jobs, intimating that we could also perform them one day when we had gained more experience.

Some of the jobs were extremely unpleasant, painful or at the very least immensely tiring. Carrying a very heavy 35" X 18" X 14" bale of compacted hay across the deep, muddy yard from the barn to the cattle shed was hell because the only practical way of doing it was by balancing it on my head. For the rest of the day, my neck would be screaming and my head pounding. Bent double, picking potatoes all day was gruelling, back-breaking work, and if we stood upright to "take a breather", George, comfortably mounted on the tractor, would shout, "Come on, boys, get on with it! This is not a holiday camp!"

Positively the worst, most disgusting task was clearing up the afterbirth when a new calf had come into the world. George averred that the best way to do it was with a garden fork—which we found perversely ludicrous—but other methods with shovels and brooms were almost as useless, as the shimmering, jelly-like mass slipped and slopped away from you in all directions. Ugh.

But many jobs were a joy to perform, and especially in good weather. Walking down to bring in the cows to milking was always rewarding. In spring, the hedgerows would be full of birds' nests, the lovely eggs shining up at you: the starling's and song thrush's bright blue; the blackbird's larger, speckled and pale turquoise; the robin's tiny white with brown spots; and sometimes the deep brown or pink of the warblers. In fall, I could gather enough mush-rooms for all our breakfasts at the farm house, and blackberries for dessert at lunchtime. And in all seasons, the sounds of birds as-sailed my ears: the *coorr-coorr* of the wood pigeon, the *caark* of the crow, the *cheep cheep* of the chaffinch, the beautiful *burblepip* of the blackbird, the high pitched chatter of the swallow, and occa-sionally the liquid *doodleoodle* of the nightingale.

On the way up to the farmyard, their udders so full their gait was ploddingly slow, each cow knew its place in the procession (the cantankerous horned Friesian Nellie Dean in the lead), and its own stall in the cowshed. At first by hand, then soon after by ma-chine, we milked them into containers which in turn we emptied into churns to be put by the roadside for the truck from Cambrian United Dairies in Marshfield to pick up.

Collecting hens' eggs was normally a job done by "the Missus", as George's wife Doreen was always known; but on days when she was tending the stall in the market, it fell to me. What a lovely hunt it was! The hens were free range in the widest possible sense, hav-ing acres on which to roam and, if they felt like it, to lay. Mostly, however, they stuck to the cowshed, the hay barn, the loft, the tractor garage, the machinery outbuildings, and a few cozy spots in the Missus' kitchen garden. Often, the eggs would still be warm, so as fresh as could be when we ate them the same day. They ranged from pure white to dark brown and every variation between, and from tiny (from the Bantams) to huge, double-yolkers.

But the most enjoyable, almost nourishing, task was ploughing. To the bystander or tourist standing on the other side of hedge, this looks effortless. They see the farmer and the tractor simply go up and down the field over and over, soon get bored and move on. But it is not nearly as simple as they imagine.

The vital functions of ploughing are the angle and depth at which the shares are set, the ability of the ploughman to vary the depth when rocks or unusual earth conditions occur, leaving enough room to turn at the end of the furrow without wasting growing space, and, above all ploughing in perfectly straight lines. If the first few furrows were not absolutely straight, you could be sure that subsequent furrows would wander all over the place, the field would look a mess, and George would be furious because he would be tormented by other farmers.

The ploughman does his work twisted in his seat looking backwards to see that the furrow maintains a perfect line. As he does this, he also sees flocks, maybe hundreds, of birds—gulls, blackbirds, crows, magpies, pigeons, sparrows, rooks—rising like billows of smoke behind him as they frantically feast on the worms exposed by the plough. To be in such a state in the evening of a summer's day is one of the most deeply satisfying, sustaining and spiritual experiences I know.

After some years, Dai and Russ moved on to pursue career training and I continued on my own until George hired a former prisoner of war who decided not to go home to Italy when peace was declared. His name was Angleo D'Angelo, a short swarthy, young man with a sunny disposition, an infectious laugh and a wonderful, uplifting tenor singing voice. As we worked away together, the fields would ring with *Ave Maria, Torna a Sorrento, O, Sole Mio, Arrivederci Roma, Funiculi Funicula*, and many more. When it rained very hard, or was bitterly cold and we took a break in the cowshed, Angelo would lower his voice and sing very softly. Occasionally Nellie Dean would join in with throaty *Mooooo*.

~

It was George who first got me interested in politics. He was incessant in his propagandizing and I was young and susceptible. He hated the Tory government of the day, denounced local government officials, sneered at religious leaders, ridiculed teachers, and maintained that all Free Masons were "on the take", an assertion he would curiously illustrate by spitting on his hand and thrusting it behind his back. He was a strong supporter of the Labour Party, saying that they believed in "fair shares for all", but my father said it was because the post war Atlee government had "feather-bedded" the farmers by giving them innumerable subsidies.

George was particularly contemptuous of Dad when he ran for County Council as an independent. "Pah!" George spat, "No backbone! He's just a Tory trying to sneak through the back door."

However, Dad always claimed he was a Liberal, not a Conservative, but voted Tory because the minuscule Liberal Party had not offered a candidate in the constituency since 1929. He said that Labour's six years in office after the war had "run the country into ground."

My own view was, and still is, that it was probably the most courageous and hard-working government in British history, but its ideologically insatiable thirst for public ownership—nationalizing railways, gas, water, electricity, road transport, coal mines, steel industry, civil aviation—was unnecessary, certainly over-ambitious and irresponsibly wasteful of resources which it could have put to better use.

One of George's heroes, later to be one of mine, was Welsh firebrand Aneurin Bevan, a former coal miner who held his Ebbw Vale mining constituency with majorities of around 20,000 votes. Known to the public from the newspapers as "Nye" (my late friend Michael Foot, who inherited his constituency, told me his pals spelled it "Ni"), Bevan was as much trouble to his own party as he was to the Conservatives, being a loud, fiery, vituperative orator who was usually unforgiving and sometimes insufferably vain.

I'll share here an amusing anecdote about Bevan and former Nova Scotia Premier Gerald Regan, about whom much more later. Jerry and I were driving along the Heads of Valleys highway and pulled into a gas station on the outskirts of Ebbw Vale. Jerry, who always claimed to be much more left wing than he really was, seemed awe-struck that we were actually standing on ground once represented by the fabled Aneurin Bevan. In a hushed, reverent tone, Jerry asked the grizzled, old gas station attendant if he had ever known the great man.

"Oh aye, I knew him well over many years," the man replied, "Worked in the pit with him. Never had much use for him, he was such a lazy bugger. I always voted Tory myself."

Downcast, Jerry returned to the car in a daze.

My first overt political act was to be campaign manager for Gordon "Gogger" Maslen, the Labour candidate in the school's mock election in 1959. Nationally, Labour was crushed by the Conservatives under Harold MacMillan, who won 107 more seats than Labour under their new leader, Hugh Gaitskill. At the school, we lost to Tory candidate Bob Llewellyn, later to be my capitalist partner in a window cleaning business which we conducted in and around the village. The Liberals were represented by class mate Karl Francis, who subsequently made a name for himself as a film director, and then for being charged with making indecent photographs of a child and of arranging or facilitating sex, causing a child sex offence. A deal was made, and the charges were dropped, but he was put on the sex offender register for two years.

On two occasions over the succeeding years, I went to see George and the Missuss when I was in the UK visiting my parents, and once saw Doreen in the small house in the village to which she moved after George's death.

Years after our first encounter, George caught me fanning the tractor with an old sack.

"What the hell are you doing?" he demanded

"Keeping the flies off the engine," I replied

George remembered, and laughed heartily.

5: Education

My first school in Wales was a two-room stone building at the end of the village, attached to the schoolmaster's house. His name was Rhys James (known as "Arry" because his initials were R.E.), a pompous martinet who strutted around like a sergeant major and constantly boasted about the attributes of Risca, the place from which he originally hailed. Years later, I lived in Risca and, apart from its having a great pub, *The Forge Hammer*, I did not find anything special about it.

Arry presided over the upper, smaller schoolroom where he taught the children aged 8-11. The lower, larger room was for kids by aged 5-8, where the matronly Mrs. Marsh ruled the roost.

I found school so insufferably boring that I recall only two incidents from this period. One was when I was cast in the Christmas play as the son of a Jewish refugee mother. My name was Gotlieb and I was directed to nibble on a piece of dry bread. It seemed I was an extra because I had no lines. Apparently, this was an indignity I was resolved never to repeat because later, in more than thirty years in film, I have never been an extra, and do not intend to start now.

The other incident involved Mrs. Marsh apparently overhearing some smutty talk and giggling (not from me), marching to the front of the class and shouting, "Tits! Tits! Tits! Are you happy now?"

Graduating to the next room and to Arry's tender ministrations, I found slightly more interesting, mainly because we did much more art, and because Arry allowed us to waste a lot of time going up to him and asking to borrow his penknife to sharpen our pencils. Another reason was that the Lovell kids attended at certain times of the year. They were gypsies who travelled in colourful, horse-drawn caravans and camped at the edge of the village. They were deeply tanned, had jet black hair, twinkling eyes and infectious smiles. Their names were Willie, Gerald and Shirley, who I think must have been my first love.

At school, I hung out with a not-too-bright boy, Graham Francis, and a braggart bully, David Tostevin, who insisted we play the game of "Let's Get..." Tostevin always named who would be got, and invariably I was the gottee, not the getter, suffering bruises and minor abrasions as a result.

When he left school, Graham went to work on a farm where, to get compensation, he deliberately cut off several of his fingers. It would not surprise me if Tostevin became a brutal mob boss.

There is not a great deal more of note to add about this little school except that it had a small playground and a garden, and that each day crates of tiny bottles of milk were stacked outside the front door. When the birds did not peck through the tin foil caps and suck out the cream, leaving specks of dirt behind, the heat of the sun turned it sour. Many years later, the Minister of Education stopped this supply of school milk and became known as the Milk Snatcher. I think the kids were better off not having to drink the filthy stuff, and I think the country was better off for having had Mrs. Thatcher.

~

I had a significant strike against me at this school in that I was not Welsh. The Welsh can be wonderful people, but their greatest weakness is xenophobia; they dislike and mistrust outsiders, and in particular they heartily dislike and mistrust the English. The more militant nationalists actually hate the English with an abiding passion, harking back to Edward I's oppression of the Welsh, to the coal and iron masters of the nineteenth century, and even to Winston Churchill's alleged (but not actual) brutality in the Tonypandy riots in 1911. Even today, some Welsh people pepper their discourse with sneering or derogatory references to England

and the English.

Some Welsh kids, especially the boys, made it clear that I did not belong there and that I should go back where I came from, although how they proposed I should carry out their wishes they never explained. The teachers were also Welsh, and scolded me when I did not know the words to *Hen Wlad Fy Nhadau* (Land of My Fathers), the Welsh national anthem, and when I mispronounced Welsh place names, as all non-Welsh people do.

Some kids would surround me in the school yard and put "itchy backs" (rosehip seeds) down my shirt, an excruciating experience I do not recommend you try any time soon. The bullies would kick me in the back of the calf so my leg would collapse, I would fall down on the asphalt and skin my knee. In the classroom, some boys who had desks near mine would cut me on the backs of my legs with rulers, snap elastic bands at my neck or flick ink-soaked pellets at me.

And some of them would tease me about "being sweet" on a particular girl. I was excruciatingly shy and would blush to the roots of my hair. Ralph Hodson, the policeman's son, was the worst and, egged on by my older brother, taunted me incessantly.

Finally, at my wits' end, I took one of my brother's darts out of the board on the wall, then lay in wait for my enemy. I dashed forward with a blood-curdling cry, plunged the dart into the boy's arm and tore away. Of course, the ramifications were quick and considerable. It was a drastic and unforgivable act, but Hodson kept his distance thereafter.

~

When we had passed our eleventh birthday, we took an examination known as the Eleven Plus. If you passed this exam—basic math, putting squares and boxes in the right places and playing "one of these things is not like the others"—you could go to Grammar School. If you failed, you could go to a Comprehensive School if you did not quit and go to work on the land or in a factory. The former was Bassaleg Grammar School, four miles away, whose motto was *Non Frustra Fatigamur* (We Do Not Strive in Vain) and was considered the school for those going places. The latter was The Graig, on the other side of tall iron railings, touted as the place for future plumbers, carpenters and electricians.

My own success in getting into Grammar School was severely blighted by the news that Dai had failed the exam and would have to attend the Graig. This necessarily meant we would see far less of each other than before, and that I would have to make new friends at my school as he would at his.

The grammar school was a large, red-brick building which occupied the crest of a rise at the end of a long driveway. By the big iron gates was a small house. I never determined who lived there, but understood it was either the groundskeeper, Mr. Grocutt, or Mr. Dockery the caretaker (janitor). Behind this house was a very large, flat green space marked out for various sports: rugby football and field hockey in winter; tennis, netball and cricket in summer.

Between the field and the school was a steep bank along which were benches which, one dark night, we foolishly and drunkenly hurled on to the field in an act of rebellion. We also ran a large pair of women's bloomers up the flag pole, broke into the Headmaster's office to shower it with whisky, and scrawled indecent pictures on the corridor walls. When the crunch came I was the only one to "own up" to the crimes, so had to suffer the punishments alone.

Bassaleg Grammar School in those days was not what today would be called "diverse" or "inclusive", but it would certainly have been representative of the catchment area—a 15-mile stretch along the coast between the outskirts of Newport and Cardiff, and some mining valley towns to the north. Of the 300+ students, I can recall none who were black or brown, and very few Jews or Catholics. During morning Assembly, when the whole school gathered, the non-Christians were allowed to stay outside while the prayer was being said, and then come in for announcements and "God Save the Queen".

The teaching staff sat in a row across the stage and the Headmaster stood at the centre behind a wooden lectern. From him we learned of coming events—a prize giving, a field day, a local fête— or of one of our number being struck down by polio, tuberculosis or a traffic accident. In such cases, we were not provided with 'counselling' or given comforting homilies, but were exhorted to maintain a stiff upper lip, and 'get on with it' in the finest traditions of the school.

Then we would sing the school song:

> *Of our school, this song we sing,*
> *Together our voices ring.*
> *As we climb life's crowded hill,*
> *The echo will linger still.*

The Headmaster was a scary, ferocious man called Penry M. Rees, who wore a black gown and gold rimmed glasses and plastered his black hair flat with Brylcreem. We knew him as "The Boss", whose terrifying approach was always heralded by the clacking of his steel-tipped shoes on the polished marble floors. When you heard this sound in the distance, you fled for your life in the other direction.

The Boss was a disciplinarian of the old school. Some of the teachers handed out "lines" as punishment (in Math teacher Ted Evans' case, you had to write out "in your best handwriting" 100 times: *Insubordination is highly detrimental to the well-being of this scholastic establishment*). However, The Boss preferred more demonstrative means of correction. In a glass case on the wall, he had an assortment of canes which, bending and swishing, he would try out in the air before selecting the one to administer on your person. He always offered a choice: "Hand or behind, boy?" and if you chose the latter, he would feel to make sure you had not inserted a protective exercise book in your trousers. Either choice was fraught with danger: If you chose the behind, he might get you on the base of the spine; if the hand, he might get you on the wrist —in both cases extreme pain was inevitable.

After being caned on the behind, sitting at your desk was torture and you had to try to sit with the head of your femur on the very edge of the seat.

Though they were never less than unpleasant, we got used to canings and some of us were beaten many times before we left school. It is a wonder my friends Ron Fisher and David Handyside could walk, they were beaten so many times. Ron (now living in Ireland) tells me he is the third most beaten boy in the school's history, first place going to an odd, turnip-headed boy called Swiddle Reid. Others who received frequent corporal punishment included Franklyn Delano Roosevelt Smith, an ape-like boy whom The Boss ordered to shave when he was only 12 years old, and John Wisbee, from whom teachers direly warned me to stay away (I ignored them).

Another lad who was caned frequently was a blond, tousle-head swimming champion, Brian Young, who lured me into collaborating with him on the production of a scurrilous, pornographic, hand-written, hand-illustrated "newspaper" which surreptitiously circulated around the school until it was so dirty and dog-eared it was no longer legible.

There were only two issues; after the second fell into the hands of French Teacher Pod Davies, we got scared and shut down the presses. Its pages contained amateurish smutty drawings and Youngie's doggerel, which he was pleased to call his "poems". Thankfully, I recall only one:

> *The Sailor's name was Harry Bell.*
> *After five bob's worth on Saturday night,*
> *His cock was red as hell.*

The gossip among the boys was that The Boss enjoyed beating us because he had been castrated by the Japanese on the Burma Road during the war. It was a salacious narrative, but none of us really believed it.

However, some years after his death in 2006, when I was searching through some documents, I came across this entry: *Gun-*

ner Penry Markham Rees, 77ᵀᴴ Heavy Anti-Aircraft RA; became POW at Garoet on Java, 8 March 1942. He had been a prisoner of the Japanese on the Sumatra railway, known as the "Pekanbaru Death Railway", where conditions were unspeakable and where the men were treated worse than animals, mercilessly worked from sunup to sundown, torture and starvation being regular features of life.

I also found a very long, poignant, Kiplingesque poem, "At the Going Down of the Sun", that he wrote about his experiences, of which here are a few verses:

> *And in spite of tropic noonday and a host of wasting ills,*
> *Ever southward went the railway to Muara and the hills;*
> *Every sleeper claimed a body—every rail a dozen more,*
> *'Twas the hand of Fate that marked them as it tallied up the score.*
>
> *On their ulcerated shoulders they transported rough-hewn wood,*
> *With a dying desperation carried more than humans should;*
> *On their suppurating feet with ber-beri swollen tight,*
> *From the rising of the sun until the welcome fall of night.*
>
> *When the Day at last arrived and when the rest of them were free,*
> *They devised a Union Jack, and displayed it on a tree.*
> *And they thanked the God who made them that He let them live again,*
> *And they prayed they might be better for the suffering and pain.*
>
> *There they left their friends behind them—thirty times a score and more,*
> *Left them sleeping in a shadow on a distant tropic shore.*
> *And I pray that God Almighty, in the evening of their lives,*

Will be gentle to their parents and their children and their
wives.

Pakan Baru SUMATRA, 1944

I wish I had known all this at the time: I would almost have been proud to have been caned by such a hero.

Teachers had their own forms of punishment, from the 'lines' already mentioned to more sadistic measures. Chemistry teacher Stumpy Stevens would grab a piece of hair just behind the ear and twist it until you squealed. Sports teacher Gilly Guildford would either hit you behind the legs with a sawn-off cricket bat or throw a heavy medicine ball at your head. Woodwork teacher Batty Owen would clip you around the head with a length of dowel rod, and once he actually threw a large bench plane at me. Had it connected it is unlikely I would be writing this today.

After what seemed like an eternity, and an extremely boring one at that, I finally left the school with six O-Level (Ordinary) and one A level (Advanced) certificates. Since the A level was in art, and because I had been reasonably proficient with Paint-By-Numbers birthday gifts, my parents thought it only natural that I should go to Art College.

So I dutifully sat the exam and passed, though to this day I do not know how.

6: Cardiff and naked women

Wales, with a population of just over three million, is about 130 miles north to south, and an average of 80 miles west to east. Its western boundary is a spectacular coastline along the Irish Sea, while its eastern boundary with England winds like a drunken snake from the Bristol Channel to the River Dee in Cheshire.

Wales has only six cities, only three of any size, and two with populations of less than 4,000. The 'big' cities, all on the South Wales coastline, are Newport, Swansea and Cardiff, of which the latter (population 320,000) is the largest and is the capital of the principality.

Cardiff Art College, when it was founded in 1865, occupied space above the public library, but two years later moved to its own premises, a rambling, red brick complex on The Friary, a road off the city's main thoroughfare, Queen Street. To a wet-behind-the-ears 18-year-old, the college looked forbidding, and inside it was a terrifying warren of corridors, stairs, rooms and workshops teeming with young people blithely dashing around, shouting "Fab", "OK Daddy-O", "Groovy", "Far out", and "I dig it, man."

Not only did they not sound like me, but neither did they look like me in my polished shoes, clean shirt and tie, pressed grey trousers and blazer. These people, if people they were, had long hair, beards, and earrings; and wore beads, filthy jeans or dungarees, ragged jerseys and dirty, old tennis shoes or "daps" in the Welsh vernacular.

I crammed into a classroom of some thirty equally-bewildered youngsters to receive a pompous, introductory homily from our "home room" teacher, a portly man named Phillip Jennings, who sported a large handlebar moustache and spoke with a "cut glass" accent. After he had finished telling what was expected of us, Jennings led us into a long room in which was a semi-circle of strange-looking benches with short easels attached to their front portion (these were known as "donkeys").

We milled around, taking whichever donkey we could get, set up our drawing boards and looked around at each other, wondering what would happen next. A few minutes later, a loud communal gasp greeted that occurrence.

From a corner of the room, her head held high, her middle-aged body wobbling, strode a totally naked woman. This was the fabled Mrs. Williams, who carried herself like a queen, but adopted poses which were distinctly and sometimes disturbingly immodest.

She nodded to Jennings, then sprawled on an ancient couch at centre stage. Some of the girls shifted in their seats and looked away, others looked down at the floor. A few students, who were directly opposite her ample bush, desperately struggled to move their donkeys out of the eye line. Some boys were squirming, some were red faced and coughing. Most, like me, just stared ahead, wide-eyed, immobile and dazed.

"Please draw what you see," Jennings intoned as he glided around the room. Noting that, even after an hour's work, a number of students had left a conspicuously white space in the pubic area, he urged. "Draw everything you see. Everything!"

In response, the recalcitrant students hastily swirled their pencils around, producing what looked more like rolls of barbed wire.

Jennings sighed loudly. "This is not the place to parade your petty, provincial morality," he boomed, "The pubes are merely a means of lubrication for an activity in which I have no doubt some of you will soon promiscuously engage. While not essential to the human form, they none-the-less appear upon it, so should as faithfully rendered as any other feature."

It did not take long for us to lose our petty, provincial morality and, at least for the boys, it only returned when Miss Woebbley visited us. Apart from the imperious Mrs. Williams, Mrs. Clode and Mrs. Davies were regular life class models. Both were in their mid to late forties and, not to put too fine a point on it, were unlikely to be recruited for the pages of *Flirt N'Skirt* or *Health and Efficiency*. However, Miss Woebbley was an entirely different and most unsettling kettle of fish.

Miss Woebbley worked for Chipperfield's Circus as some kind of performer (trapeze artist, I think) and sat for us as a life class model only at certain times of the year. She was young, she had a beautiful face, and had a body which could only be described as spectacular. The problem was that half the boys spent the two hours just staring, while the other half experienced acute discomfort as they shifted and squirmed in their seats. When Jennings once casually, evilly, draped a small silk cloth over her shoulder, the writhing and groaning became audible.

Once, fortunately only once, we had a male model, Mr. Sotheby, a dirty, saggy, paunchy man in his early seventies who claimed to have had a career on the stage and who announced from the platform, "I've had my women...*and* my men." During his breaks, instead of retreating to the corner for a cup of tea as the women did, Sotheby would stroll around the room, looking at the drawings and leaning over the students, making sure to rub his naked body against them.

It was abundantly evident from his street clothes that Sotheby was as poor as a church mouse, and as much as he repulsed us, we took pity on him and at the end of the session invited him to join us in the pub for a pint. He threw up his hands in horror.

"Forbear, young sirs, forbear!" he wailed. "How dare you insult one such as I in this manner. Begone, I say, begone!"

Another example of no good deed going unpunished was when we took pity on another indigent visitor. He was a tall black man who used to sneak into the men's cloakroom to wash his legs and feet in the sink. We christened him 'Orrible 'Erbert, and when we similarly invited him to have a pint with us, he grabbed his battered shoes and ran away down the street at breakneck speed.

When I say "we", I mean the gang with whom I hung around. Gareth Jones is now a Professor at Rhode Island Art College, Clive

Bowen is a successful potter in Devon, and the last I heard of Jack Crofton, many years ago, he was working in a foundry in London. The whereabouts of bubbly Robbie Robinson and joker Leighton Williams are unknown. Many times I have tried to track them down, but every lead was a blank.

Also unsuccessful were my efforts to locate Carolyn Porter, with whom Gareth and I fancied we were in love. She was tall, with doe eyes and a sad face. She made it clear that she was not interested in either of us. Sometime later, I met her again, when she told me that she had indeed requited my feelings and had told Gareth as much. To this day, he flatly denies this. I shall never know the truth of the matter, and this many years later the only consequence is unsatisfied curiosity.

In addition to life drawing, we studied linocut, etching, painting, pottery, sculpture, and calligraphy under an assortment of oddities who called themselves lecturers, of whom I can recall David Tinker, Joan Baker, Geoff Milsom, Frank Roper, Eric Malthouse, Frank Vining, Kitson Towler, and the principal, J.C. "Jack" Tarr. Of the latter, Jennings would irreverently chant:

> *Twinkle, twinkle J. C. Tarr,*
> *How I wonder who you are.*

Jack was a small, stiff martinet with a black moustache and a military bearing who was seldom seen in and around the college. But when he did appear he seemed like a malevolent spider creeping the corridors.

I have only two anecdotes about Jack Tarr. One was when there was a student uprising over recreational space, and a strike was threatened. Jack, speaking quietly to the wall above their heads, addressed the students. If they wanted a strike, he said, they were welcome to it. In fact, he strongly encouraged them to strike. If they did, he said, nothing would please him more because he would not have to deal with such unpleasant people, and because it would save the college a lot of money and enable him to balance his accounts.

The other occasion was when he deigned to perform in the annual college concert (a flattering term for a raucous and unruly event). He stood there like a stone statue and in a barely audible tone sang *Frankie and Johnny* with such ill grace we thought it must have been a calculated insult. The applause was negligible and came only from the staff.

A member of staff I liked, who was not a teacher but a sort of technician, was Joe Friede. In addition to being an all-purpose handyman, Joe mixed the huge amounts of clay required by the sculptors and potters. Then he had to add "grog"—gravel, broken shards of fired pots, and sometimes sand—to the clay to make it less liable to crack went it eventually went into the kilns. This activity and the man who conducted it were considered to be the lowest of the low, even by students who came from the roughest of working-class families. The relevance of this will become apparent a little later.

Of all the lecturers, my favourite was Geoff Milsom, a small, mild-mannered Yorkshireman who had been born in the same town as the great Henry Moore, attended the Royal College of Art, and come to teach at Cardiff in 1950. He was self-effacing, soft-spoken and tentative, but always kindly and helpful. He would run his fingers over everything, almost as if he were blind and this was the only way he could determine the form of an object.

Perhaps it was not surprising that Geoff was my favourite (and his fellow Yorkshire sculpture lecturer, Frank Roper, my second favourite) because, above all other kinds of art, sculpture appealed to me most. It still does, but while I have been able to execute many paintings in the ensuing years, very seldom have I been able to do any sculpture because it requires a large space where cleanliness is never a requisite. While inspiring and invigorating, sculpting is invariably messy, dusty and sometimes filthy.

Once, when my friend, the late Professor Leslie Alcock, had discovered a small, stone head (likely from the early Christian period) on an archaeological excavation, I took Geoff up to the university to see it. The crudely-formed head sat in a box of sand in the middle of the room, and Geoff circled it several times, bobbing his head and peering through his glinting spectacles. Hesitantly he reached out, as if he might break it, gently touched it and then pulled away. Then he moved closer and, almost enveloping the sculpture in his arms, gently stroked all surfaces.

He told Leslie that the head had not been carved, that no tools had been applied to it, and that it had been wrought solely by abrasion. Leslie professed himself deeply grateful and, later, incorporated Geoff's analysis in his report.

I am sorry to say that the others, Crofton, Evans and Jones in particular, had less respect for Geoff than did I, and tended to see him as a failure. They reasoned that if he were a really good sculptor he would not be teaching in a provincial college, and they saw his mild-mannered, soft-spoken ways as apologetic timidity.

Once, Geoff invited us up to his house, a place which was as understated and modest as Geoff himself. We sat around drinking tea and then went out to the garage to see his latest work.

"The garage!" Jones whispered in incredulous disgust to me as we shuffled down the side of the house in the dark. "*That's* his studio?!"

When we got inside, Geoff switched on a hanging light bulb and invited us to squeeze past his little car to the work bench. There we saw two or three little soapstone carvings, none taller than eight inches. I thought them charming and well done, but the others gaped, then grimaced at each other behind Geoff's back. On the way home in the bus there were no limits to their ridicule. I was profoundly saddened.

I was even more saddened when I went back to Cardiff some years after I had moved to Canada. By then the college had moved to a new location across town, so I parked my car and navigated the sparkling corridors, trying to find the sculpture department.

Eventually I located it and stood before the notice which listed the names of those who taught there. Geoff's name was absent. I could not understand it because he would still only have been about fifty, so I accosted a man who was walking past me and asked him.

"Milsom? Ah, yes, I think I know who you mean," he said. "He's down in the basement. Go down the stairs to the bottom and go right to the end. You'll find him in the Grog Room."

My mind reeling, I followed the directions and sure enough, in a dank, windowless room, there was Geoff covered in dirt, pounding the grog into the clay with a heavy spade. He didn't know who I was. He told me he had suffered a stroke a year before and had completely lost his memory. He could remember nothing, not even his family and, of course, he had lost all knowledge of art, sculpture or teaching. They had let him stay on doing the grog as an act of charity.

On my way back, I had to pull the car off the road to dry my eyes. He died in 1976 at 59.

As we have seen, it was while I was at Art College that I became involved in archaeology, getting away to excavations ("digs") around Wales whenever I could. Often, the dates of the digs would clash with a sculpture session, and when I asked Geoff if I could go to the dig, he would always give me this infuriating answer: "I'll leave it your conscience".

As often as not, I flew away to the hills to dig, which, no doubt, is one reason why my working life went to archaeology rather than art.

Another reason was that, at that time, I was utterly useless as an artist. I could not understand why, and none of the lecturers ever said the words which might have helped.

They told me other things which were deeply valuable and have stayed with me all my life, most importantly that if one looks carefully at the world around, one derives infinitely more benefit from it than those who drift through life barely noticing anything which is not directly in front of their faces. This is the single most significant lesson I learned at college, and for which I have been eternally grateful. It taught me to *observe* rather than merely see. Many, many times over the years, I have been with others, particularly outdoors, when I have mentioned some fascinating item—a tree, a cloud, a bird, a building, a person in a window, a passing vehicle—

which they had not noticed. (You can educate yourself in this re-spect by walking down the main street of your own town looking up, rather than ahead. You will be amazed at what has existed there without your ever having known it.)

The other influential thing I retain from College actually came from Jennings, who was usually given to pompous sententiousness. He once leaned over my board and said quietly, "Most art should be 90% looking and planning and only 10% making marks. Sadly, with you, Akerman, I see it is the other way around."

That wisdom did not sink in properly until much later, but it has proved its worth over and over. Whereas many painters sit before the blank canvas in solemn silence and tentatively proceed at snail's pace until the work is completed days, even weeks later, I finish my own paintings quickly—often in a few hours. That is be-cause I have spent days thinking, planning and looking. When I am before the easel I know what I want because I can see it in my mind.

That was much later, not when I was a student. My problem then was that I spent all my days at college trying to produce work which was like someone else's—a famous artist's or another stu-dent's—and/or concentrating on techniques and gimmicks instead of getting down to the heart and soul of the job at hand.

Had Geoff, Frank, or any of them simply said, "Don't worry about what others are doing or what they think: Just be yourself," my time at college would have been much more rewarding, and pos-sibly my life might have taken some very different turnings.

7: Digging up the past

My introduction to archaeology came when a school chum, the late Adrian Lewis, told me a Society was being formed in Cardiff, and suggested we go to the founding meeting. It was at the Royal Hotel on St. Mary Street, where there was an enormous carpeted lobby (which also served as a bar) with large, circular tables and huge, sink-into armchairs.

Around one of these, the new Cardiff Archaeological Society came into being. The founding members were Adrian; myself; Peter Green, an effeminate man from Blackwood in the Sirhowy Valley; Frank Hennessy, an affable Irishman serving in the Royal Navy; and the convener, who turned out to be a fraud, poseur and all round utter shit. He proposed himself for president and someone suggested I be secretary. The motion was carried, and we were in business.

Our president called himself Frank Ryan-Jones and he spoke with a posh upper class accent. However, his real name was Tom Jones, from Splott, one of the roughest working class areas of Wales. His mother's maiden name was Ryan and his middle name was Francis. Later, when he discovered that we knew about his background he would frequently say, "My family is a source of considerable social embarrassment to me."

As obnoxious as he was, he was relentless in his efforts to advance in the archaeological world and in his pursuit to be regarded as a member of the area's minor aristocracy. He was also persistent in his exertions to impress upon us his undoubted masculinity ("my genitals are of great size and weight," he once said to me in a serious, matter-of-fact way), relating his multitudinous sexual adventures with beautiful young women, some of them well known in the media. Much later, on the eve of my emigrating to Canada, I learned that his inclinations were actually in quite a different direction, and that he and Peter (whom the others were unkindly calling 'Miss Green') were something of a notorious item around the city. This, of course, was several years before the Sexual Offences Act legalized homosexual activity between consenting adults, in 1967.

Our first dig was on a supposed medieval earthwork at Cottrell in the Vale of Glamorgan, where several trenches produced almost nothing. Then we moved further west in the Vale to what was thought to be a fortified manor at a tiny village called Llantrythyd.

We spent several years excavating here, finding masses of 12th century pottery and a little ironwork. Then, suddenly, the site was almost awash with silver coins. They were "short cross" pennies from around 1130, during the reign of Henry I. Consultation with the professionals indicated that these coins were the contents of a scattered horde, a hidden stash which the hiders had never retrieved and which was later disturbed. With all due pomp, we transported the coins to the British Museum in London and handed them over to the tender care of Dr. Michael Dolley, to whose name were impressively appended the letters D.Litt (Lond), MIRA, FSA, Hon. D Litt. (NUI).

One fascinating feature of many of the pennies is that they were not perfectly round, but had portions missing. This, we learned from Dr. Dolley, had been caused by the King's moneyers clipping bits of silver, melting them down and making more coins than authorized. The king exercised severe punishment upon the miscreants, including in some cases amputation. In 1125 he ordered that "All the moneyers in England should be mutilated" by being castrated and losing their right hands.

The discovery of coins naturally enhanced Jones' celebrity and ego beyond all endurance, and some of us left the Society to join other digs or conduct our own. One group, which my late friend John Beare led, were so incensed by Jones's posturing that they committed the unforgivable act of descending upon the site by night and desecrating it. It was widely believed that I was a party to what became known as the "Attack from Vandal Ridge", but I was not, and a few days later left for Canada.

Other archaeological excavations in which I participated in those years, included Deganwy Castle in North Wales, post-medieval platform houses at St. Harmon in Central Wales, both directed by Leslie Alcock; and several wraths, or earthen ringworks, in Pembrokeshire, directed by David Crossley. In later years, when on vacation, I also did some digging for a very old friend, Steve Clarke, in and around Monmouth, an ancient town in the southeast of Wales, hard on the border with England.

The excavation at Deganwy was most memorable for a number of reasons. The weather was wonderful, always important to archaeological diggers because there is nothing so miserable and soul-destroying than scraping away in the earth amid howling winds and torrential rain.

The site was in the medieval castle which is perched on the top of a steep hill overlooking the Town and River Conwy to the north, the Great Orme promontory to the north, and the Irish Sea to the west—as spectacular a location as could be imagined. The castle had been built in the thirteenth century, but we were looking for the citadel of Maelgwyn Gwynedd, the 6th century King of north Wales, which legend said lay beneath the medieval structure.

We conducted the dig in three areas, of one of which Leslie Alcock put me in charge of, which was a very satisfying statement of confidence in my knowledge and ability. There was a large, cheerful gang of students from the University of Wales, Bangor, some 17 miles away, including the daughter of the Chief of Police in Bermuda, a very tall, very black, bright, bubbly girl who was always guaranteed to lighten the mood and get us laughing. And there were Mary Williams and Barbara Thomas from the south Wales coal valleys and Dennis Harding, a posh, jaunty chap studying at Oxford University. Harding owned a car, something which in those days was impossible for most people and certainly for anyone under 30.

Harding's car was the supposed scene of an alleged disgraceful event—one which never actually took place, but which people surmised from circumstantial evidence. We had been on a pub crawl of the Conwy Valley one evening and ended up walking out on the Great Orme in the pitch black. Scrambling through the gorse, Mary fell and cut her knee.

When we got back into Deganwy, Dennis dropped Babs off at her B & B, but it was too late to go back to the guest house where Leslie, Mary, I and most of the crew were staying because we did not have keys. Dennis drove to his hotel and, parking in the lot, told us we would have to spend the night in the back seat of the car, which we did.

All you need to know about that night is that Mary was as chaste as a nun and that her wounded knee bled on to the car seat.

In the dawn's early light we crept along the streets and back into the guest house. On the way we encountered Leslie out for his morning newspaper. He raised his eyebrows and formed his lips into a silent whistle.

Later, on my way up the long hill to the site I noticed that people seemed not as friendly as usual and a few shook their heads at me in apparent distaste.

The mystery was solved mid-morning when Dennis came charging up to my trenches, shouted,, "You cad! You utter bastard!" and them stormed away downhill.

When I turned to my site assistant and asked what it was all about, he hesitantly explained that the word was all around the dig that Dennis had seen the blood and deduced that I had deflowered Mary Williams on the back seat of his car! Mary had to go to Leslie and tell him it was all nonsense, and Leslie put a stop to the gossip as best he could.

8: Working for a living

For reasons outlined in a previous chapter, I failed my examinations at Art College. Today, I have no doubt I could pass that exam with flying colours because, while I had extensive knowledge then, I had no wisdom, a commodity I suspect comes only with experience, and mostly unpleasant experience at that. I knew what had to be done and how to do it, but was unable to put it all together and make it work for me.

To an extent, it was similar when I was a politician in that, while I could give stirring speeches and knew how to get re-elected, I was naive to an extraordinary degree in dealing with others in the political sphere, believing that whatever they told me was sincere and true. Here again I had knowledge but little wisdom.

Today, I am what is called "a quick study", but assuredly I was not one when I was young. Only with the passage of time did I gain a real understanding of politics, but by then it was too late.

As my father's fortunes had taken disastrous turn, my failing the exams meant I was out in the world on my own and without means of support. My first job, as a teacher at a private school, lasted one day. They told me the teacher who was leaving, and for whom I was supposed to be filling in, had "changed his mind". Whether this was true, or (as I suspect) they took one look at me and decided I would lower the tone of their establishment, I shall never know.

~

The next job was allegedly as a "colour consultant", which was how the position was advertised. It was with a large Cardiff firm, Rapports, which had a number of branches, retail and wholesale, in clothing and furnishings, and was managed by various members of the family known as Mr. Morrie, Mr. Cecil, and Mr. Hymie. I think it was a young Mr. Cecil who interviewed me for the post, explaining that the job entailed assisting customers buying carpets, curtains, couches etc. to co-ordinate their purchases so they would not "clash" and leave them disgruntled. However, Mr. Cecil said, in order to do my job properly I would need to have a "broad knowledge" of the products they sold, and in order to do this I would start in their carpet and linoleum warehouse on Womanby Street, a Rapport subsidiary called Bingham's.

Naive youth that I was (and would remain for a very long time), I signed on the dotted line and buckled down to obtaining a "broad knowledge". A host of names of products and types —Dunlopillow, Axminster, Dunedin, Walton, Congoleum, Nairn, Crossley, Tomkinsons, Brinton, Carter, Pilkingtons, Craven Dunill—come flooding back. I recall that the best, thickest and most expensive carpets were rated AO, the leanest, cheapest A3.

In addition to carpets, Bingham's specialized in linoleum, tiles and rubber underlay which were packed into the four stories of the warehouse which were linked by a rickety, hand-pulled, rope-operated, wooden elevator.

Humping large carpets, boxes of tiles and rolls of linoleum around was a living hell, and hauling the loaded elevator up to the top floor, hand over hand, was an exhausting, back-breaking ordeal. If you slipped and loosened your grip, you could tear the skin off your hands and the loaded cage would loudly crash into the stone ground floor, spilling contents across the foyer and into the street. All this was rendered all the more unpleasant because the warehouse itself, built in the 19th century, was appallingly hot and filled with clouds of dust.

After months of waiting for a call from Mr. Cecil to assume my duties as Colour Consultant, I finally realized I had been duped. They had been unable to fill the vacancy by truthfully advertising the real title of the job (warehouse labourer) and its duties, so had resorted to subterfuge. In a rage, I stormed through Rapport's main department store, into the office and told Mr. Cecil what he could do with his job.

That made me feel good—for about an hour. Then I realized I was again without the means of eating and paying rent.

~

Shortly after leaving Rapports, I ran into Frank Roper, who was head of the sculpture department at college, and when he told me he needed help in and around his house and studio in Penarth, a seaside resort two miles away, I immediately accepted.

Frank had invented what became known as the Lost Polystyrene Casting Process which he used in a foundry attached to his garage. Here he had a large work bench, a furnace, a ladle and a wide variety of tools. He glued blocks of polystyrene together, then carved out his forms and surface details in the foam. We then covered the sculpture with burlap mixed with plaster and, when it was dry, poured molten metal into a hole in the top. As the metal burned the Styrofoam it displaced it, so that the finished product was an exact replica of the original, but in aluminum or bronze.

The main problem was that as the metal encountered the foam it gave off a disgusting, sickening, dense black smoke which choked us and sent us running out into the yard, gasping for breath. Frank would cough for a while, grin widely, then light up a cigarette.

Other jobs I did for Frank and his wife, Nora, included laying a concrete driveway from the road to their garage, and building several brick walls. Bricklaying requires more skill than one might imagine and it takes time to learn the basics, but after a few wobbles and collapses I got the hang of it and did a creditable job.

There can be few pursuits as thoroughly satisfying as building a wall. Certainly, bricklaying is repetitive, but seeing your efforts translate into a growing, tangible result is intensely rewarding.

One hideous sensation from that time stays with me. For most people the misophonic event of fingernails on a blackboard is their greatest abhorrence, but for me it is the horror of handling a dusty paper bag of cement. Today, I think they call it "Tactile Defensiveness". Ugh!

After a few weeks, Frank sadly informed me that he had no sculpture commissions lined up and that no further work around the house was needed, so I was on the street again.

~

After a sober evening of thinking, I recalled that when I was a teenager I had worked on weekends at an aluminum factory in Rogerstone, only a mile or two from my old school. So I called Joe Dudley, the sub-contractor, and got hired on as a labourer in the Services department of Alcan Ltd., a Canadian company, then headed up by the wartime hero, General Viscount Alexander of Tunis.

Of course, lowly labourers did not rub shoulders or clank tea cans with the likes of Lord Alexander, or indeed with anyone from management. Our bosses were foremen called "charge hands" whom we feared and from who we incessantly tried to hide.

One was a slimy, bald little man, Steve Lewis, who wore a long khaki coat and rode a bicycle around the plant. He claims a corner of my memory chiefly because he once told us that if someone put a newborn German baby in his hands he would dash its brains out on the concrete floor. But even more feared was the dreaded Shyers, a cranky old bear of a man who snarled and had the knack of appearing out of nowhere.

The primary and re-melt furnaces were fiercely hot and roared loudly. I both dreaded and was fascinated by these Mordor-like hell holes and greatly admired the half-naked men who toiled there.

One week I was seconded to the bricklayers who relined the furnaces with white refractory bricks and, while I really liked the brickies themselves, getting inside a dusty furnace, which had only been switched off days before, was not my idea of fun. Temperatures inside must have been around 35°C. We could only stay inside for a few minutes at a time, and drank gallons of water each time we struggled out.

At lunchtime, the brickies became inveterate, almost fanatical, gamblers, betting on anything and everything. At our table, an average lunch break would sound something like this (at that time, before decimalization, a "bob" meant a shilling, or one-twentieth of a pound. Half a crown was a silver coin worth two shillings and six pence):

"Alright Bill, bet you ten bob that fly don't reach the ceiling."

"You're on!"

"Lenny, bet you two bob the next person comin' in the room is an 'oman."

"You're bloody on!"

"Idris, bet you half crown Ted Prosser puts spuds in his next mouthful."

"Alright, you're on!"

I kept the tally and announced who owed what to whom before we returned to the furnaces.

As a result of working on the furnaces, I did something of which I am heartily ashamed. I cannot imagine where my brain must have been. A bricklayer, a nice guy called Brian Williams, said he wanted to make his wife jealous. He asked me to fake a letter to him from a Madame Zenobia, saying all manner of complimentary and salacious things about him.

May G-d forgive me, I agreed and not only penned this offensive missive but even splashed some of my mother's perfume (she called it "scent") on the paper. Apparently, Mrs. Williams received the letter in the next day's mail and, when Brian came home, beat the living daylights out of him with a rolling pin and forced him to reveal my identity and address. The letter she wrote me was furious, vicious, disparaging, excoriating, belittling and totally deserved.

The Extrusion section was equally fascinating. There, a much smaller, round ingot was heated until almost molten then punched through a steel die with an enormous hammer. The white-hot metal would exit the mould cavity in the form of a very long, narrow pipe along a guided trackway until it was coiled. If one of the guide blocks came loose, the pipe would snake out of the trackway and shoot up into the roof where, hitting the struts and beams, it broke up into dozens of small, triangular, still-hot pieces. When this happened we would run like lightning for cover.

It was while in the Extrusion Department that I caught a snatch of conversation which produced one of those lines which, once heard, are never forgotten. As I was carrying equipment past a group of men, I heard one say, "I can hold my piss, but the man who can hold his shit is dead."

Services department covered everything from disinfecting the offices, to plate-laying on the company railroad (which had many miles of track), to cleaning toilets, to painting pipes, to cleaning under the continuous rolling mill which stretched for almost a mile. I performed all of these functions at one time or another and can say, without hesitation, that toilet duty was by no means the most unpleasant. That distinction went to work under the rollers.

The continuous mill comprised maybe as many as 20 sets of presses, each exerting more pressure than the previous one, and hundreds of rollers. At one end an enormous white-hot ingot would enter the mill. As it glided over the rollers it became thinner each time it went through a press until, at the far end it became aluminum sheeting, used for siding, roofing, making cans and many other purposes.

To reduce the heat from the ingot and from friction with the rollers, a constant stream of thin oil was sprayed on to the rollers and, when the ingot went through the presses thin pieces of metal were shaved off and fell through to the greatly elongated pit below. These pieces, known as swarf, formed into sharp spirals and came to rest in three to four inches of oil. It was our job to slide under the rollers and, on our hands and knees in the filth, the hot dripping rollers just above our heads, remove both swarf and oil. For the first hour or so our work gloves offered protection, but the swarf soon ripped them apart, and after several shifts on this duty, our hands were not only greasy and black as night but also covered in ugly cuts.

The most pleasant, though often dangerous, job was working on the railroad which ran around, through and in and out of the factory. Because much of the track was outside the main activity, and among shrubs and long grass, we were often unsupervised, so could occasionally sit in the sun and listen to yarns from Reg Snead, a wiry little Welsh butty who had been there for years and who instructed me on how to lay sleepers, shovel-pack beams, attach fish plates, bolts and shoes, and bend rails with a deadly apparatus called Jim Crow.

This latter was a semicircular iron bar with "claws" at each end and a long threaded bolt through the middle. When we needed the track to curve we would insert a rail in the claws and turn the bolt until the rail had bent to the required degree. If The Jim Crow slipped, with a loud thwang the rail would spring out and fly through the air. If it caught anyone or anything, as it occasionally did, the results were gruesome.

In those days, getting from Cathedral Road in Cardiff to the factory was a major undertaking requiring walking about a mile to the bus station, getting a Newport bus, then changing to a Cross Keys bus to Rogerstone, but it could be done if I was on the afternoon or night shifts. However, when I was put on the morning shift, I had to be there at 6 am, before the buses started running, which meant I had to leave around 4 am and hitchhike all the way. Some days it worked out, but other days there was either no traffic or no driver willing to stop. So, I had to quit.

~

Years before, Dad had been general manager at Dialoy, a non-ferrous foundry on Colchester Avenue in Cardiff. The factory did mostly die-casting of aluminum and bronze products for large orders, but also had a sand foundry for smaller or specialty items. I remembered that the company Secretary's name was Frank Davies. So I went into a telephone box, called him and gave him a sob story. I was very lucky that he hired me on the spot ("for old time's sake" as he put it) and the next day I went to work in the sand foundry.

There, we fabricated aluminum products, like pulleys and doors for railway cars, by carefully making an impression with a wooden pattern in dark red silica sand contained within a large, steel box on the floor. (Sometimes called "green sand", silica sand was mixed with a little bentonite clay, and, unlike regular sand is dense, silky and holds whatever shape to which you fashioned it.) Then we would impress the other side of the pattern into another large box of sand. We very gingerly removed the pattern removed, dusted the sand impressions with iron oxide to prevent cracking and metal penetration, and fastened the two boxes together. Then, when the metal was molten and at the right temperature, it would be gently, but continuously, poured into the mould.

The men would stand back and silently pray for success because, mysteriously, there was never certainty as to what might happen inside the mould when the metal and sand made contact. After a suspenseful wait, we unfastened the boxes and knocked the casting out. If it was perfect, it was a joy to behold, and the men cheered loudly. But if something went wrong, they loudly cursed and swore, hurling tools and sometimes their boots at the offending casualty.

A faulty cast was called a "shitter", and was very bad news for the moulders because they were paid by piece-work, not by the hour, so would lose money and would have to do the whole thing over again, sometimes taking an entire day.

I loved it from the minute I set foot inside the large, barn-like building which had a dirt floor and a high roof under which a gantry crane could slide from one end to the other. Six moulders and their labourers worked in this space, while at one end was the foreman's office and a large, cluttered room where a dishevelled man called Charlie made the cores and patterns.

I was labourer/assistant to Mostyn, one of the more experienced moulders, a small, quiet, confident man whose expertise was fascinating to watch. Mostyn was a consummate craftsman who very rarely cast "shitters". It was an honour to work for such a skilled perfectionist, and there have been few people in my life for whom I have had more admiration. On the other hand, the fore-man, Ted Lloyd, was a red-faced, kindly man, but was disorganized and shambolic, mixing up orders and frequently rescinding in-structions.

So, before I left Dialoy to go to Canada, I told Frank Davies that I thought Lloyd should be retired and that Mostyn should be the foreman. Some time later I was highly gratified to learn from Dad that this had transpired, and I like to think I was at least partly re-sponsible.

9: Off to Canada

When I assisted Leslie Alcock in excavating medieval platform houses in Radnorshire, I had met Bruce Fry, who was one of his students at the university. Bruce, who hailed from Watford in the south of England, was a bouncy, pipe-puffing little fellow with whom I became friends for a short period, after which he disappeared from my scene.

Then, shortly after Christmas in 1963, I received a letter from Bruce informing me that he was now an archaeologist with the Fortress of Louisbourg restoration project on Cape Breton Island in Nova Scotia. He also said that the project, run by the government of Canada, needed someone to head up their research illustration department, and since I had both archaeological and artistic experience he was authorized to offer me the job.

The remuneration was $5,000 per annum (about $42,000 in today's purchasing power), plus low rent housing. Since I needed work, and had no plans or prospects, I accepted.

In early 1964 I boarded a BOAC 049 Constellation at London Heathrow, and after what seemed like an eternity—my recollection is about 7 hours—disembarked at Gander, Newfoundland. The most distinct memory of the flight is that at dinner we were served Cock-a-Leekie soup.

At Gander, I waited almost all day, sitting around and trying to translate the loudspeaker announcements into the language I spoke. I was particularly fascinated by the announcer's way of saying "Easterrrn Puvinshul Hairrrways". Eventually the connecting flight to Sydney, Nova Scotia, arrived and I humped my suitcase on to a Vickers Viscount, another propeller aircraft carrying about 30 passengers.

In those days, Sydney airport was not much more than a large barn with a squat tower on top. On the front was painted *Department of Transport*, and underneath *Sydney* and *Canada* with a maple leaf in between. It was bitterly cold and dark, the only illumination coming from the windows and a tall, gloomy yellow lamp.

What drew my attention most were the enormous mountains of snow heaped up around the building and perimeter. The wind howled across the concrete. "Oh G-d, what have I done?" I asked myself.

I passed through the "terminal" and out into the night, where I stood shivering until a short, fat man wearing khaki coveralls and a yellow hard hat waddled up to me.

"You the Limey?" he asked.

I acknowledged that I was.

"Get in the Fargo," he grunted, indicating the back doors of a large black van bearing the words: *Government of Canada, Department of Indian Affairs and Northern Development, National Parks Division.*

As he shuffled to the front of the van, I opened the back doors and got in. There were no seats, so I sat on my suitcase, which made me knock my head on the roof when we went over large bumps.

The journey from Sydney to Louisbourg was interminable, and as I peered out of the small windows could see only snow: deep snow on the road, thick heavy snow on the trees, and ten-feet-high banks of snow on either side. Later, I learned that snowfall in Cape Breton that winter was the highest since 1941. As we sloshed, swished, swerved and skidded those twenty miles that night, my heart sank lower and lower.

It did not lift when we arrived at the fortress, then only snow-swaddled earthen banks, two stone buildings and the snow-covered, concrete beginnings of the reconstruction of a bastion. The Fargo slid to a stop outside the stone building and the driver grunted: "This is you".

I stumbled out and he drove away, spraying me with snow. It

was pitch black, the only light coming from one of the windows. From the sea, only a hundred yards away, the wind slashed across the open ground like a razor, whipping streaks of snow from the crests of the banks.

I saw that the smaller stone building was a dwelling and the other, in total darkness, a museum. So I staggered to the house and pounded on the door.

Bruce opened the door, casually muttered, "Oh, so you're here then?" and told me where to put my coat and suitcase. He then ushered me into the kitchen where the other occupants of the house were gathered around the table.

They were: Edward McMillan Conyors Larrabee, the Senior Archaeologist, a very serious, almost surly man who was a native of Washington State; his equally lugubrious beagle Bolivar; Iain Walker, a tall, bearded Scot who stuttered; and Peter Harrison, a willowy American who had excavated at Ti'Kal in Guatemala.

The next day they took me into Sydney—which to me seemed like some town out of a cowboy movie—to buy a parka and some overshoes. Here I had my first, but by no means last, experience of learning to converse with Cape Bretoners. In the store, when I stated (clearly, I thought) what I wanted, the clerk said what sounded like, "Waby? Yoffabo?"

After several attempts at communication, Edward intervened to explain that in Cape Breton people were addressed as "B'y" and that the clerk was asking me if I was "off a boat" because it was clear I was a foreigner.

Having obtained my heavy coat and ungainly rubber overshoes, we crossed the street to the London Grill, an airy, quite smart restaurant, where much gingham was in evidence, both in the waitresses' uniforms and the tablecloths. I had Kentucky Fried Chicken, coleslaw, Grecian bread and fries, only the last of which I had ever eaten before. I thought it was wonderful and the height of luxury.

For quite some time, I was equally enamoured of other "luxuries" which were entirely new to me, like frozen mixed vegetables, fish chowder, corn chowder, scallops, capelin, lobster, pizza, Iron Brew, spruce beer, corned beef and cabbage, white rum, moonshine, salt cod and scrunchions, hot meat sandwiches, waffles, Sweet Marie and Cherry Blossoms.

~

There was another archaeologist on the team whom I did not meet until the some days later. He did not share the stone house with us, but rented a broken-down cabin at Catalone, some miles away. This was Don MacLeod from Toronto, who was to become my close friend. Don was a tousled, squint-eyed, shambling man who chain smoked, drank heavily and would fornicate with any woman who would have him, regardless of age or appearance. In these respects, Don was very like another friend and colleague, Buddy MacEachern, whom we shall meet in a later chapter. Don and I spent all our evenings together with various local families, at bootleggers or, in summer, at the bunkhouses where the student site assistants lived.

Don took his guitar everywhere and sang, so he could be guaranteed the centre of attention, especially since his songs were often, to say the least, unusual. A few I remember were: *I Don't Care If It Rains or Freezes, Got My Little Plastic Jesus; Honey Have a Sniff on Me; All the World is Desolation* (with the names of those present in the room inserted into the lyrics), and *Saint James Infirmary*.

Frequent hang-outs were at the house of Tom and Dorothy Lynk in town, and at Tom's brother Danny's place near the Fortress, which was known as "The Sugar Shack". Tom was a hard-working man who had little to say, but Dorothy, an Acadian from Cheticamp in northern Cape Breton, was loud, bubbly and fun-loving. She loved to drink, dance, laugh, and sing *Quand le Soleil dit Bonjour aux Montagnes.*

Wisely, Tom retreated upstairs when it got late, leaving Dorothy to kick up her heels with us downstairs. These "parties", in reality little more than extended drinking sessions, often petered out just as dawn was breaking.

At the Sugar Shack, things were somewhat different, being

rather sad and depressing because both Danny and his wife Toot-sie were alcoholic and frequently were shaky and verbally incoher-ent. They were bootleggers, selling quart bottles of Moosehead beer at slightly over the price charged by the Nova Scotia Liquor Commission, which had a total monopoly on all kinds of liquor. Sometimes, there would be as many as ten people crowded around into the house, smoking, drinking and listening to Don's singing. Frequently, one of the customers would be Wynn Parsons (known as "Wint") who played *Wildwood Flower* on the "cordeen" until he collapsed on the floor.

At a certain point in the proceedings, Don and Tootsie would disappear behind the burlap curtain, which separated the living area from the sleeping quarters, from which unmistakable sounds emanated. If Danny, who was seldom alert, knew what was going on, he never showed any sign of it.

~

The restoration at Louisbourg was a project of the Diefenbaker government, and was designed to offset high unemployment caused by coal mine closures. Louisbourg was first settled by the French in 1713 and the Fortress was built between 1720 and 1740. New Englanders besieged the Fortress in 1745, and the British in 1758.

The project, originally estimated to cost $26 million was con-ducted by four main departments, subject to the overall direction of Project Manager Dave Perry, although we used to say that his secretary, Sandy Ferguson, really ran the show. Fussy, uptight, bur-eaucratic Reg Glencross ran Administration; Research (including archaeology) was under the urbane, sardonic Fred Thorpe; Engin-eering under no-nonsense Larry Vachon; and John Lunn, an ingra-tiating Englishman who later became Park Superintendent, headed Interpretation.

A strange collection of misfits and what Don called "social refugees" from all over the world headed various sub-depart-ments. The best of these was John Dunton, a wonderful, kindly gentleman from Virginia who was in charge of conserving the finds, and who had a large collection of Baroque records. It was he who introduced me to Vivaldi, something for which I will always be grateful.

Others included Edward Larrabee; historian Carmen Bickerton; Head Draftsman Henry Van Der Puten an irascible, overbearing Dutchman; stonemason John Urich; and a hulking fellow called Olson whose job was to oversee wrought ironwork. This latter, elderly, unprepossessing character ended up with the tastiest, most voluptuous teenage site assistant, Ryder Johnston, who, we learned, was granddaughter to one-time Group of Seven painter, Frank Johnston.

Construction, under Larry Vachon's watchful eye, had a cast of weird and wild characters, none more colourful than Norman Lanctôt, who boasted of feats and accomplishments which were clearly impossible (he once claimed to have slid an entire cathedral into place using grease as a lubricant)' Kippy Shaw the foreman; and Blacky Brown, who operated a gigantic earth-moving machine.

T. Marmon "Smitty" Smith from New Brunswick and his right hand Al MacNeil from the coal mining town of Dominion ably oversaw the archaeological field operation. We archaeologists each had site assistants, including the large, bubbly Urve Linnimae; Richard Wilcox; teasing Terry Tailor; dour Sue Kardas (whom Larrabee later married); snotty Lynn Soucie (who married Iain Walker); Elizabeth Wylie; Renee Marwitt; and an utter pain in the ass called Dimitri, who would never follow an instruction, always responding, "Vell, maybe, vee'll see."

A host of labourers included the irrepressible Alex Cameron, Neil Cox, testy Mike Ferguson, my wife's uncle Black Jack the Rat MacDonald, Frank Hickey and Gervaise Wadden, these last two once threatening me at knife point on Kennington Cove beach.

The colour of the hard hat you wore announced and preserved the hierarchy. White hats were bosses—department and sub department heads, and archaeologists. Technical personnel like photographers, and surveyors like Pat Cormier who was also a great fiddler, word blue hats. Foremen had red hats. All others wore yellow hats. One advantage of this class system to the labourers was that they could see a boss coming half a mile away and stop gossiping or smoking well before being caught.

I had adequate quarters to set up my operation in the Administration Building, in a compound back in the forest, and as much equipment and material as I wanted. It seemed money was no object to the Government of Canada, and all I to do was order what I wanted and it duly arrived.

At first, I worked on my own, then later acquired draftsmen/women, including Andre Grenier and Lucille Lepage from Quebec and an older, infuriatingly-difficult German woman, Herat Maerch.

No matter how often I tried, I could not drum into this little virago's brain the fact that we had to keep in mind that all drawings of archaeological finds, when published, would be greatly reduced in size. This meant that the original drawings needed to be bolder and heavier than normal so their contents would be clearly visible when they appeared in scholarly publications. Herat assiduously ignored this, using the finest pens and most delicate lines to reproduce the objects she was given. Even when I got Charts and Drawings department head Hugh Gilmour to reduce her work and showed her the pitiful result, she refused to relent, defiantly declaring, "Vee shall see vat Mr. Larrabee sinks of zis." Unfortunately, Edward only made things worse by soothing her ruffled feathers and piously expressing the vain belief that we "would work things out."

After a year heading the Research Drafting unit, I became an archaeologist and went out into the field, where my esteemed site assistant was the aforementioned Richard Wilcox, a likeable, intelligent Nova Scotian with whom I remained friends for many years. Together, we excavated a number of buildings in the interior of the fortress, the reports on which are likely still gathering dust in some government basement.

Soon Americans Joe Vogel (with whom I am still in touch) and Dick Lane, who, though young, had been an Elector for the State of Wyoming, joined our archaeological team. Not until much later did

Dick bring his voluble and volatile wife, Rikki, to Louisbourg, but from the outset Joe's wife, Jeanie, and their utterly charming little daughter, Amber, accompanied him. Later still, more Americans, Jervis Swannack and Jack and Renee Marwitt, joined us.

For a while, two British archaeologists worked with us. They were a huge, extraordinarily eccentric man called David Sturdy and his voluptuous but rather snooty friend Helen Sutermeister, one of whose claims to fame was that her grandfather had been an admiral in the Swiss navy.

Sturdy had written to Edward expressing an interest in Louisbourg, so when I went back to Britain to see my parents, he asked me to interview Sturdy and, if I was favourably impressed, to hire him. I met him in the Ashmolean Museum in Oxford and the deal was clinched over a pint in a local pub.

The Sturdy-Sutermeister team did not get along well with the other archaeologists because they were considered high-handed, and because they used earth moving machinery (including Blacky's enormous Dominion) instead of trowels and brushes. When Sturdy would shout, "Hack it out, Blacky!" Fry would wince and the others would roll their eyes.

Archaeological excavations can be very laborious and frequently boring, and since I would not want this narrative to be likewise, will give just a few anecdotes of interest from those years.

Around the inside walls of the King's Bastion at the fortress was a series of walled compartments called casemates, in which the soldiers performed various duties and which in time of siege temporarily held the injured and dead. Excavations here were difficult in winter because the frozen earth required hours of thawing from large blast heaters; but when we got going, we discovered all manner of artifacts, including many bandages employed by the French soldiers to bind their wounds.

We treated these like any other finds, often using the same hands which blew noses, rolled cigarettes and held sandwiches. Imagine our horror when weeks later we got the scientific reports back from Ottawa, informing us that the bandages were crawling with live Tetanus bacteria some 207 years after the last siege. It was extremely fortunate, if not miraculous, that none of us developed any symptoms!

The main building of the King's Bastion contained the Chapel St. Louis, and when we excavated there, it soon became apparent that many corpses were buried beneath the floor. The skeletons were of some small children and various officers and officials. One of them was of the Governor, Jean-Baptiste-Louis Duquesnel, who died there in 1744, a year before the first siege.

The scientific boffins' report on his skeleton revealed a wide range of horrible illnesses which contributed to his death and which must have made his life a living hell for years: he had lost a leg in combat, and suffered from arthritis, arteriosclerosis, and dental abscesses, the decay having eaten its way into his jaw and up into his skull. The historical records indicate that Duquesnel was a cranky, difficult man to get along with, and it is no wonder considering the degree and length of his suffering.

For some reason, Edward Larrabee formed the rather condescending view that local people would believe that gold was buried with the bodies, invade the fortress at night, and ransack the site. He instructed us to get ground sheets and sleeping bags and spend our nights in the chapel until the excavation was complete. This was an uncomfortable inconvenience, but apart from a few jokers pretending to be ghosts, there were no memorable incidents. To the best of my recollection, we found no gold.

The Fortress project occupied a number of separate sites in and around the town of Louisbourg: the fort itself on a large, forlorn, windswept promontory; the administration building in the woods; a conglomeration of bunkhouses and a canteen for the students, also in the woods; various tourist interpretation centres known as belvederes, a housing area of good, substantial dwellings for the married officials; and a trailer park for mid-level employees, to which I moved when I left the stone house, even deeper in the woods. Mac and Mora Esterbrooks, Norm and Eleanor Lanctôt, model maker Calju Hinrikus and the wonderful painter, Gerald Roach, who died in 2009, also lived at the trailer park.

~

Some months after I went to Louisbourg, I formed a friendship with a woman whom I would meet in the forest halfway between the housing area and the trailer park. Following several of these nature walks, I developed a large lump in my groin, so went to the local doctor for assistance and advice.

Thorny Mosher was his name, and local gossip said that one should never see him after 2 pm as he would then be too drunk to be coherent. Fortunately, I got there early, paid my $5 fee (this was before Medicare) and was duly examined.

"You've got a dose," Thorny announced.

"Oh no!" I cried. "You must be wrong. What else could it be?"

Thorny took down a number of medical tomes from his book shelf and leafed through them.

"Got any ingrowing toenails?"

"No," I replied after hauling off my socks.

"It's a dose."

"Must be something else."

Thorny turned more pages. "Stepped on any metallic objects?"

"No," I told him after having removed my shoes and socks a second time.

"It's a dose," he said firmly.

As I sat there in a daze, I started scratching my chest.

"Why you scratching?" Thorny demanded.

"I was bitten by blackflies in the woods."

"Blackflies!" he shouted, "Of course, that's it, blackflies! There's your answer. They carry *Oncohocerca volvulus*, which infects the lymph nodes."

As I left, greatly relieved, Thorny flashed a huge grin. "Close one," he said.

When I got home, I called my friend thinking she would find the story highly amusing, but when I related it I only got as far as Thorny's initial diagnosis. She abruptly hung up. I did not hear from her again, and did not see her for another 34 years, when she was an extra on the "Pit Pony" TV series shoot in which I played Frawley, the mine manager.

~

It was at Louisbourg that I first became involved in Canadian politics, and in so doing met two families who were extremely kind to me: those of James and Jean Harte, and Bill and Allie Skinner.

It came about during the federal election of 1965, when Dick Lane; his crazy wife, Rikki; Clarence Saulnier, who worked in the Interpretation department; and I went for a pizza at the Napoli on the Esplanade in Sydney. While we were there, we saw a poster advertising a rally that night at which national New Democratic Party (NDP) Leader T.C. "Tommy" Douglas would be speaking on behalf of local candidate Ed Johnston.

Dick suggested we attend, so we scoffed down our pizza and raced across town to the venue.

Given my background with George Clease and the Labour Party in Wales, I guess I did not need much converting, but Douglas was spell-binding. His words and unique delivery inspired us to get involved as soon as we could.

Over the years, Tommy Douglas became a great friend, even being sympathetic and understanding when, years later, I had to leave the party. He told me that he too had once, although temporarily, "lost his faith", as he put it. He was kind, a brilliant orator, and was full of wit and fun. One day, he asked me if I knew the difference between a cactus and a caucus. When I said I did not, he said: "With a cactus, all the pricks are on the outside."

After the rally, we trooped over to Ed Johnston's campaign headquarters to volunteer to help with the campaign. It was there I first met a strange man, a teacher called Paul MacEwan who was to play such a huge role in my political life for the next 15 years.

We discovered that Louisbourg was in a different constituency, where an Allan Bragg was the candidate, so we returned home armed with leaflets, ready to hit the streets for him. In those days, New Democrats in Louisbourg were as rare as hens' teeth, but among the very few were Jimmy Harte and Bill Skinner, who contacted us and pitched in.

On Election Day, poor Bragg was utterly slaughtered, coming a dismal third with only 427 votes. Ed Johnston did somewhat better, but also came third.

It was in that campaign that I first gained experience of the corrupt practices which had characterized Nova Scotia elections for a century and would continue to do so for at least another decade. To get an idea of the enemy's strength and tactics, I attended the Liberal Party rally at the Navy League Hall on behalf of incumbent Allan J. MacEachen, who became immensely powerful in the national government and something of a folk hero to those who received his many hand-outs of taxpayers' money. As they filed out of the hall, MacEachen and town Mayor George Lewis asked each person If they wanted a "job at the park", meaning on the Fortress restoration project. I said I already had a job at the park, so they unceremoniously ushered me out, but some thirty to fifty people asked for, and were told they would get, these jobs.

I cannot say if all who were promised were actually rewarded, but between the next day and the election, the site seemed to be crawling with men in yellow hard hats.

~

In 1966 I was asked to go to Colonial Williamsburg, Virginia to see the Director of Archaeology, Ivor Noel Hume, with whom our Conservator, John Dunton, had worked prior to his coming to Louisbourg. The purpose of the trip was to see if I was suitable to fill the position of Assistant Director at the famous restored town, which the Rockefeller Foundation funded.

When I got there, I loved the place, and Noel and I got along exceedingly well. He offered me the job at a handsome salary and a rent free, restored house in the town. As the well-worn expression has it, I thought I had died and gone to heaven.

When I was asked to meet with the board of the Rockefeller

Foundation, I thought it was to be a formality, a confirmation of Noel's decision. It was indeed, but there was an enormous proviso in the chairman's ominous words: "And your job will be waiting for you when you get back."

I must have looked bewildered, because he added, "We have checked with the Draft Board and you are 1A, so you will have to go to Viet Nam."

I had not realized that non-citizens had to fight for the United States if they lived and were employed there, so my dreams were dashed. They were most understanding at my reluctance to visit South-east Asia under those circumstances, put me up in the Williamsburg Inn for a few days and gave me a credit card to use in the town. Noel later told me that they had given me the nickname "Cannon Fodder".

Another adventure I had in the United States happened as a result of Dick Lane's wife, Rikki, inviting me to accompany her on a drive from Louisbourg to New York City in her Austin Healey convertible. Rikki was, to say the least, an unusual woman, being a heavy drinker who was demonstrative in word and deed. She thought nothing of grabbing any man, at any time, and planting a huge wet kiss on his lips; and at dinner parties or card games she would often loudly address her husband: "Richard, I'm getting horny. Get rid of these people."

It was the dead of winter, with thick snow on the roads, but I was foolish enough to accept her proposal. The journey was a nightmare, not only due to atrocious weather, appalling road conditions, and the car having so little ground clearance, but also because I was suffering terrible pain from a root canal infection.

Rikki, who did all the driving, continually drank beer the entire way. As she swerved and skidded, she cursed and blasphemed, often blaming me if she ran out of beer or when she got stuck in snow banks.

How we got to New York and into Manhattan I shall never understand, but we eventually made our way to Sullivan Street, off Washington Square, where an old boyfriend of Rikki's, Vincent, had a tiny one-room apartment. I slept on the floor under the table, while they shared the small bed.

Since Rikki was almost always drunk, every night started with her fiercely shouting and cursing at Vincent, arguing with him for an hour or more, then making-up with very loud sex.

I loved New York City, and was amazed that some businesses stayed open all night, and that the street scenes were exactly as I had seen them in dozens of movies. It was a very different place in those days from the lawless hell hole I believe it is today, where criminals are released without bail to repeat their crimes, and where Jews are openly and viciously attacked in the streets. We walked freely in Central Park at night, and once took the whole day walking from the Lower East side, through Chinatown, Little Italy, Midtown and Harlem up to Sugar Hill. Not only were we totally un-molested in any way, but did not witness one act of violence or law-breaking.

Vincent worked for a publishing company so was occupied dur-ing the day, so Rikki and I bummed around the city sight-seeing. After the first few days, I left them to their own devices in the evenings, ate at various delicatessens (what wonderful places, what sights, what smells!) and then more often than not would wind up at the No Name Bar on Hudson Street. There, a tall bar-tender, Jay, presided over a nightly game of charades, ordering the customers into two teams. If anyone declined to obey his instruc-tions, he would hurl ice cubes at them while the bar owner, who looked just like Frank Sinatra, strolled around quietly asking people if they were having fun.

One night, I didn't feel like going to the No Name, so I wandered around the streets, finally finding a place where the clientele looked infinitely more prosperous and better dressed than I. Since nobody stopped me, I went in and, seeing the only empty seat alongside a grand piano, sat down and ordered a Dewar's on the rocks from a very nervous looking waiter.

Soon, to thunderous applause, a large, black, middle-aged man with a pencil moustache came in, grinned broadly at me, sat down and started to play and sing songs which were vaguely familiar to me. He was a great performer and was very friendly towards me. As I was leaving, the nervous waiter asked me how I knew the black man. I said I didn't and had no idea who he was.

"Jesus, I thought you guys hadda be buddies," he said. "That's Fats Domino."

After some days, Rikki decided she was going to drive to Albuquerque, New Mexico, where she had friends and relatives. I decided I could not possibly endure such a journey, so begged off.

Vincent and I were warning her not to go alone, when a delivery truck pulled up and a young black man got out and took a parcel into a store. When he came out, a pouting Rikki stuck out her chest, went up to him and asked him if he wanted to go with her. Amazingly, he said "yes", and took off to get his things from his apartment not far away.

I got out the atlas and worked out a route for them, which, because of the racial complexion of the south, had to go due west to Wyoming, then due south through Colorado. It surprised me that this added only about 300 miles and an extra day to the trip. I have never seen, or heard from or of, Rikki since that day.

~

Some months after I got back from New York, I learned that Indian Affairs and Northern Development would not be renewing my contract. I do not know for sure how/why this came about, but I suspect that Bruce Fry and his friend John Lunn (who had become Park Superintendent, replacing Dave Perry) were central to the decision, and that my political activity with the New Democratic Party was also influential.

Fry had become very hostile towards me since I mentioned at a staff meeting that the people who worked for me had difficulty understanding him because he mumbled. Fry snarled, "You arrogant cunt. You are not here to do what you want to do; you are here to do what we tell you!"

I had not had any particular problems with John, but he was widely known as a man of many faces. A lasting image of him is of one night at his house when he was sitting on the floor at the feet of the Deputy Minister, Ernest Côté, gazing adoringly up at him like an obedient dog.

Tommy Douglas raised the matter of my dismissal in House of Commons in Ottawa, but the minister, Arthur Laing, brushed it aside, saying that I had obviously spent too much time "digging up the past."

10: Into the fray

Following my departure from the Fortress of Louisbourg, the Nova Scotia NDP reluctantly appointed me as a part-time organizer for Cape Breton. In reality, the work was full-time, but the pay was so "part-time" it was sometimes non-existent, as it depended on a few contributors chipping in from time to time. Had it not been for the extraordinary kindness of Bill and Allie Skinner in letting me have free bed and board at their home in Havenside, I could not possibly have done it. It is hard to imagine such lovely, big-hearted people, and all the more so because they both worked at the local fish plant, so were by no means rich.

My work was pretty much confined to Cape Breton County, as the party was utterly dead and had only three recorded supporters in the other three counties of Victoria, Richmond and Inverness. I drove around in a gas-guzzling, V-8 1950 Buick, signing up members, accepting meagre donations, and prodding people to hold meetings, elect officers and prepare for a provincial election, which we expected any day.

Cape Breton County had a history of electing leftish/labour members, having elected three such members to the Legislature in 1920, three in 1941, two in 1945 and 1949, one in 1956 and 60, and a Member of the national Parliament from 1945 to 1957. However, Robert Stanfield's Conservatives had come to power provincially in 1956, and John Diefenbaker won nationally a year later. So, when I came on the scene, the Tories were very much ruling the roost, and the NDP was disorganized and despondent, morale being so low that most of the members who did not express themselves as being tired and worn-out, told me I was wasting my time because there was no hope.

However, a very small handful of devotees inspired me to keep going, and I pay tribute to their dedication and assistance, especially to Paul MacEwan, Evelyn Murphy, James Harte, Bill Skinner, Charlie Palmer, Agnes Bates, John L. MacKinnon, Gerald Yetman, Murdock Matheson, and Al Clarke. I do not know if Evelyn is still with us, but all the others are gone.

In May, 1967, Premier Stanfield called a provincial election to be held May 30, two days after my birthday. Louisbourg was in the Cape Breton West constituency, where neither the NDP, nor its predecessor the CCF, had ever done well, so there was nobody angling to get the nomination. Encouraged by Bill Skinner, Jimmy Harte, Douglas MacDonald and Doug Roberts, I stood for and was acclaimed as the candidate.

My speech to the sparse crowd was, apparently, lacking in policy but full of flowery, emotional imagery. A version of a speech I delivered all over Cape Breton at that time, it began: "The rivers of hope have run dry."

The local weekly, the *Cape Breton Highlander*, attacked me, describing me as a youngster with "Messianic tendencies". This was not to be the last time that the paper's publisher, Sandy Campbell, would excoriate me: He kept up his barrage of invective for another nine years until the paper went out of business.

The other NDP candidates in Cape Breton County in 1967 were Paul MacEwan in C.B. Nova, Gerald Yetman in C.B. North, Tom O'Leary in C.B. Centre, Charlie Palmer in C.B. South and the party leader, James Aitchison, in C.B. East (where I was to be elected three years later).

Running Aitchison, a Halifax professor, in a coal mining constituency was an audacious notion and a huge risk. I confess the idea was mine, and I persuaded the party brass that since C.B. East offered the best chance of electing someone, it made sense that the leader should run there.

I doubt any NDP candidate could have succeeded there in 1967, but in the event, Aitchison campaigned in a didactic, patronizing way, his wife even offering to adopt some "poor" children they encountered while canvassing. Sometimes, Aitchison got lost in his speeches, often saying "Great Britain" instead of "Cape Breton" and in one speech repeatedly called for a new *flishpant* to be built at the wharf.

Aitchison lost by 2046 votes to Tory incumbent Layton Fergusson, MacEwan by 1044 votes to another incumbent, Pinky Gaum, and I was slaughtered, coming third with 1178 votes to the winner, Ned Manson, who got 3862. The others also did poorly.

~

I was never sure why, because he and his partner were confirmed Liberals, but shortly after the election, Ron Neima, owner of CHER Radio in Sydney, asked me to become a news reader and host of a nightly phone-in show. The team I joined there included co-owner Bob McGuigan, Dennis Natalona (known on the air as Natal or The Ukrainian Cowboy), Jack Columbus, Weldon Boone, Ron Roswell, Jim Lovelace, Ronnie MacLeod, and technician Norm Robar.

Jack was a fine fellow, Weldon was great fun, Dennis was strange but friendly, Ronnie was pleasant and easy to get along with, and Norm was enigmatic and rather greasy. The others I would not have trusted for two minutes, and would certainly not have gone tiger hunting with them.

The phone-in show, called *Night Line*, aired from ten until midnight. Neima recorded a ridiculously pretentious introduction to the show in which, to the accompaniment of dramatic music, he declared: *"Night Line! The voice of an island, a province, a nation.... and a world!"*

When the *On Air* light went on I was completely on my own, as we had no delay system (to allow the controller to delete obscenities before they went out), and nobody screening the callers before I took them. The consequence was that frequently drunken callers came straight on to the air cursing and blaspheming, and once a woman continued to argue her point as she was fighting off her husband's physical advances. "Jerry b'y, the old man's trying to get into me," she told the world, "I told him he hadda wait till I finished listening to your show."

In retrospect, I can easily see why the show was seen in some quarters as irresponsible, not only because obscene and foul language could not prevented, but also because I encouraged listeners to bitch and complain about anything and everything and, in particular, to be critical of anybody in authority at any level of government. I fear I was, in fact, a rabble-rouser.

However, the show was immensely popular. Neima informed me that our ratings were many times higher than television in the same time slot.

Over a period of weeks, the same caller, local union representative Gilbert McIntyre, repeatedly asked me why there was no union at the radio station. Then, Cape Breton was highly unionized and non-union employers were regarded as evil or "scabby".

Knowing that Neima monitored the show from his home, I made circumspect responses to McIntyre, but this set in motion a series of events which ended my sojourn with CHER.

An organizer from the International Alliance of Theatrical Stage Employees, Moving Picture Technicians, Artists and Allied Crafts of the United States, Its Territories and Canada contacted me and asked me to sound out the other employees. I agreed and did as he asked. Only a few were interested in having a union; most, being scared for their jobs, were hesitant and non-committal.

The upshot was that Neima quickly got wind of this and, not too politely, invited me to leave the premises, never to return. A federal Labour Department bureaucrat held a few so-called "conciliation" meetings, which were fruitless, but he declined to take any action against the station.

IATSE made me a Life Member of the union, but I was out on the street again.

~

I hardly had time to look around for new work, though, because the 1968 federal election came upon us and I was chosen as the

NDP candidate for the constituency of Cape Breton East Richmond. There had been redistribution since the previous election, but the new constituency was still favourable to incumbent, Tory Donald McInnis, who had thrashed our candidate, Ed Johnston, in 1965. McInnis was a former coal miner who was known as a tough scrapper and a formidable opponent.

The nominating convention at the Central School in Glace Bay was the first time I met Allan O'Brien, the guest speaker, who was Mayor of Halifax. He was one of the few well known people in Halifax who supported the NDP and, as he was a wealthy businessman like his friend Lloyd Shaw (whose daughter later became the party leader), he was treated as the party's sugar daddy to whom all major decisions had to be deferred. A fuzzy, rather cerebral and patronizing man, he was later to be one of the leaders of the anti-Akerman faction within the party.

There is little about the 1968 campaign which was especially memorable except for a dynamic speech by broadcaster and later senator Laurier LaPierre at one of my rallies, and for the wonderful kindness of Joe and Mary Matheson who let me live at their house on Rosewood Street in Glace Bay: this gave me an address in the constituency. I should also mention that I had recently met and was seeing a New Waterford girl, Anne Marie White, who later taught me that no good deed ever goes unpunished.

On Election Day, I was again slaughtered, coming third with 7,749 votes to McInnis' 11,583. My fellow candidate in the neighbouring constituency, Steelworkers' Union president Martin Merner, suffered an even more ignominious fate, securing only 3,426 votes to the Tory winner's 14,971.

Not long after the election, Anne Marie informed me that, prior to meeting me, she had conducted an affair with a married teacher in New Waterford, was consequently pregnant, and asked me to help her. I contacted a historian friend, Selma Barkham, whom I had met through the Louisbourg restoration project, because she had once told me she helped "girls in distress."

I agreed to drive Anne Marie to Quebec (she telephoned her mother with the bad news *en route* in rural New Brunswick), where Selma had found her a place with a family not far from Aylmer. There she was to remain until her child had been delivered and, I presumed, placed for adoption. The only subsequent communication I had with her was a nasty message just after my election to the Legislature two years later.

I had failed again to achieve my political ambitions, was out of work once more, and was a thousand miles from my adoptive home, Cape Breton Island.

~

Once, at Louisbourg, I had been so low that I had contemplated suicide and had called the first clergyman in the phone book. He came up to my trailer in the woods immediately, and thereafter became a great friend. He was Rev. Bob Knight, the United Church minister, who was so outspoken and controversial that his parish kicked him out of town. His open support for me in the 1967 provincial election certainly did nothing to endear him to the conservative congregation.

He and his family, wife Kay, daughter Barbara (who called me not long ago to let me know that her mother had died), and sons Bobby and David had accepted a call from the United Church parish at White Lake in the Ottawa Valley.

To them I went for shelter and succour, staying with them for several weeks until I had outworn my welcome and had to move on.

It was at that point that I contrived to meet my first wife, Joan MacKinnon. Those events occurred as I have described them in the first chapter of this book.

While I was living with Joan in Ottawa and working part time for CBC Radio there, I received a letter from Paul MacEwan, informing me that the Nova Scotia NDP was to hold its annual convention in Cape Breton for the first time in many years, and that, as a result, many Cape Bretoners who had previously been unable to afford to go to conventions in Halifax would be now be able to attend. Paul suggested that these could be favourable circumstances in which to challenge the hold on the party the "Halifaxers", as he always called them exercised. In particular, he said, it might be possible to unseat Aitchison as leader, and he urged me to consider the attempt.

Aitchison's leadership had been ineffective for some time, and I later described it as "academic and indistinct", a characterization to which he took violent objection and to which he furiously returned time after time in weekly columns which the Liberal *Cape Breton Highlander* was only too glad to provide for him. Even some "Halifaxers" had privately complained to me about Aitchison, not least of them the party Secretary, Peggy Prowse, who at one point urged me to consider going for it, something which was ironic in light of her virulent opposition to me later on. Others who had encouraged consideration of leadership change included Dalhousie professor Keith Jobson and Lloyd Shaw.

In view of the unwritten rule that it was mean and ungrateful to challenge an incumbent leader, Joan and Paul agreed with me that I was unlikely to defeat Aitchison even in Sydney, with full delegations from the United Mineworkers and United Steelworkers unions in attendance. But we felt we had to do something to shake up a party which at the time commanded a mere 5.2% of the vote and showed no signs of making any real effort to gain more support. Paul said that if I would run for Leader, he would go for the party Presidency.

The deal was forged.

So, from Ottawa, I issued press releases indicating my intention, and in Cape Breton Paul went to work lining up support. In my announcement, and in all subsequent releases and speeches, I made it clear that I was running on the platform of full time, paid leadership. Aitchison, a professor of political science (a contradiction in terms if ever there was one), had very much been part time, surely one reason why the public and the media alike did not take the party seriously. I said that the leader had to continually travel the province, give speeches, and attend functions and events everywhere, but that in order to be able to do that he had to receive an income from the party.

Paul reported that, as expected, the miners were 100% in support, and most of the steelworkers were also on board; but unexpectedly, many Cape Bretoners, including prominent union people, expressed hostility. Among these, Paul advised, were Gilbert MacIntyre of the Canadian Brotherhood of Transport and General Workers (the man who had started the trouble at CHER Radio), Allister MacLeod of the Canadian Labour Congress and Donald Steele of the United Steelworkers.

What Paul called "The Old Guard", people who had held constituency offices or party memberships for a long time, but had been effectively inactive, joined them. Paul said these included Duncan MacKay, the provincial party president; Violet Thorne; Nelson Muise; Aubrey Farrell; and John MacAskill;

Paul told me that party members from New Waterford, Dominion, Reserve Mines and Glace Bay were virtually unanimously on side, and in Sydney we had Ed MacKinnon (my father-in-law), his brother Walter, Tommy Walsh, Bernie Galloway, some members of the extended family of Forman Waye who had been elected on the Labour Party ticket in 1920, and, I think, Gilbert McIntyre's bother Lorne and his amazing wife Ritchie.

Even so, we knew that with the Cape Breton "defectors", as Paul called them, together with almost total support from the mainland constituencies, Aitchison would win fairly comfortably. But the effect, we hoped, would be that the party would put more Cape Bretoners on the executive and council, would wake up, and finally get serious about politics.

Then out of the blue came the announcement from Aitchison that he would not re-offer for the leadership. He did not give any convincing reasons, but took the opportunity to make it clear that I was a thoroughly dishonest and dangerous blackguard.

This changed the water on the beans and gave us some encouragement, because it indicated that Aitchison figured he might lose if he stood again, and because we would no longer be up against the power of incumbency.

Hard on the heels of Aitchison's announcement, the already-mentioned Professor Keith Jobson declared that he would be standing for the leadership. This surprised me in light of Jobson's previously expressed sentiments, and because he seemed too hesitant a person to want to be in the spotlight. A lawyer originally from Saskatchewan, Jobson was a small man with a high pitched voice and nervous gestures, but I had always liked him.

I formed the impression that Keith had been pressured into this action. In any event, the entire party establishment and Old Guard came lumbering out of the woodwork to support him and, with each passing day, our prospects seemed less encouraging.

Joan and I had driven down from Ottawa and stayed at her parents' house in Sydney, where, at time of writing, her amazing sister Barbara still lives. As he was about most political matters, her father Ed was gloomy about our prospects, cheering us up with reports of this and that person expressing opposition. He explained that it had to do with my full-time, paid leadership platform because these people were saying that *they* would have to pay for it.

Of course, this was nonsense because nobody could force them to donate to the party and, truth to tell, most of them were not donating anyway. But it proved a powerful influence on the delegates and I am sure it had swung more than a few votes away from us.

The convention took place in the ballroom of the Isle Royale Hotel on Dorchester Street in Sydney. As soon as Joan and I entered, I knew that even should we win we were in for some horrible times. The atmosphere was so poisonous you could have cut it with a knife.

Worse, Keith's slogan was *JOBSON FOR UNITY*. Its message was clear: It meant that if he won, they were sure my people would lick their wounds and get behind the new leader; but that if I won, his people would fold their tents and quit the party. The venom on the floor was palpable, and it seemed that everyone was totally committed one way or the other.

Canvassing was pointless since only supporters wanted to be seen talking to me and hardly anyone wearing a Jobson button would even speak to me unless to say something nasty or insulting. Gilbert McIntyre said to me, "You are D-E-D. Dead!" and Aitchison careened around the floor like a madman, spewing bile wherever he went.

However, Paul told me there was a group of young people representing the New Democratic Youth who were uncommitted. They were Bob Lyons, Chris Thurrott, Ken Clare, and Kim Cameron. I had a lengthy meeting with them, attempting to answer their questions as best I could. I doubt I was particularly impressive or convincing, but I learned that when they met with Keith he had been testy and patronizing, so that might have given me an edge.

On the final day, Keith was ushered into the hall by plaid-attired pipers and polite applause from the Old Guard. Just as the pipes subsided, one of my supporters, Murdock Matheson, was heard to say, "Get on with it b'y. We've had enough wind blowing through glens."

In his speech, Keith waved his arms about, stressing that he was not some stuffy academic but, as he put it, a "horny-handed son of toil." The stolid looks on the faces of the miners and steelworkers suggested they were not convinced.

When it came to my turn, I was determined to make the point that, while I had at least a fighting chance in Cape Breton East (Glace Bay), there was zero chance of Keith being elected in Halifax because he had received only 4% of the vote in the previous election, and no NDP candidate in that area had achieved more than 600 votes. So, after a few opening pleasantries, I asked rhetorically: "Glace Bay, can we do it?"

They leapt to their feet with a resounding "YES!"

"Halifax," I then asked, "Can *you* do it?"

There were a few weak, barely audible responses, which made my point far better than I could myself.

Just getting warmed up, I was preparing to lambaste the Liberals and Tories, when amazingly the chairman, party President Duncan MacKay, cut me off, saying, "We've heard quite enough of that. You sit down now." If there were any delegates left on the fence, his arrogance and bias pushed them in my direction.

When Mackay, who appeared to be almost in tears, announced the result, I had won by four votes. The New Democratic Youth claimed that they had put me over the top, but we shall never know.

My own view is that, had Aitchison run again, he would have been handily re-elected as leader, and that his realizing this pushed him over the edge and was responsible for his subsequent vehement, almost insane behaviour. I also think that on opening day, the Jobson forces had it in the bag, but their own tactics pushed a sufficient number of delegates in my direction. In any event, the battle was not over: It was, as Churchill said, not even the beginning of the end, but only the end of the beginning.

Having sat in a hot ballroom all day, on hearing the result of the leadership vote, the miners made a beeline for the local taverns to celebrate. This removed about 30 delegates from the floor, resulting in the Old Guard winning all Executive positions, including the presidency, which went to a puffy-faced, holier-than-thou teacher, Burris Devanney. This, in turn, meant that the governing Provincial Council was heavily anti Akerman, our side having representatives from only six constituencies (as there were no party organizations in Victoria, Inverness or Richmond), while they had the votes of the president, past president, vice president, secretary, treasurer and the representatives from about half of the remaining 30 or so ridings (the others also being inactive).

The Council met after the convention wrapped up, and from the opening gavel, their naked hatred for me was unmistakable. The message was clear: The convention had made a gravely serious mistake in electing me Leader, and while they could not vote me out until the next convention in two years' time, they would not co-operate with me in any way and would make my life as uncomfortable as possible.

In order to maintain their control of Council they soundly defeated a motion which would have given each of five affiliated unions a representative, despite the fact that these unions were, to a large extent, financing the party. And they brushed aside the fact that I had run and been elected on the platform of full-time paid leadership, saying that if those who had voted for me wished to pay me they could do so, but the party as such would not. They knew that the meagre donations from working class people in Cape Breton could not sustain the proposition.

Later, even when we got a few more supporters on to council, they further fudged the issue by establishing a separate Leadership Fund from which the leader would be paid, but to which contributions were strictly voluntary.

It would be tedious for the reader were I to relate the innumerable ways in which this brought suffering, stress and hardship upon Joan and myself. Suffice it to say that relying on the handouts of generous but mostly poor people meant that we never knew if we could pay the rent or buy groceries. At one point, it was so bad that Joan had to get work in Halifax to allow us to pay our bills.

It was while she was away that I accidentally came across a letter from her mother telling Joan that she should never have married me because I could not provide for her as a decent husband should. I cannot describe how empty and desolate I felt. It was one of the worst moments of my life.

This situation lasted two years and, though, as we shall see, finances were almost as strapped after I was elected as they were before, although once I became an MLA I had a small but guaranteed income. After I left politics, it took me ten years to pay off the debts I had accumulated during the ten years I was an elected member.

I spent the two years between winning the leadership and the provincial election of 1970 fending off the unceasing undermining tactics of the "Halifaxers"; trying to keep body and soul together; travelling the province to set up constituency associations; and canvassing in Glace Bay, signing up party members, and drumming up small donations. In these efforts, I shall be forever indebted to the work of, and support from Paul MacEwan in particular, but also the late Henry MacDonald, Alex MacPherson, Frazer Steele, Murdock Matheson, John L. MacKinnon and, of course, Joan.

I had set up a little office in the front room of the old half duplex we rented on Phalen Road (where, upon going out one morning, I found my neighbour's dead body), and there I saw constituents, listened to their complaints and problems, and took their cases to various government ministers and bureaucrats. As I shall later relate I was not a huge fan of Nova Scotia's bureaucrats, at least not as they were during the Buchanan premiership; but in the early days there were outstanding exceptions, most notably Ivor Hambling of the Department of Welfare, later Social Services, later Community Services (the insidious disease of Political Correctness was already under way), who paid diligent attention to every case I brought to his attention.

One of the talking points I used in speeches and in TV appearances during the subsequent campaign was that the sitting MLA, Tory Layton Fergusson, sat in the Legislature and received the stipend, but I was doing his work for him. This was not as unfair as it might at first glance seem, because while Layton was a nice man, he was lax in constituency work and was a professional lawyer, which meant that inevitably there was a fuzzy area where legal services and political representation became confused.

In passing, I might mention that, some years later, people fiercely excoriated Paul MacEwan for asking for some remuneration for a lengthy Workers Compensation appeal case he had undertaken for a constituent. MLAs who were also lawyers could have done likewise without any reproach or criticism. But then, as now, politics is full of hypocrisy.

In late 1969 or early 1970, I attended a function at Port Tupper at which Premier G.I. Smith was cutting a ribbon for something like an expansion of the pulp mill, or maybe the first foundations for the future power generating station. I was very much an outsider, and almost certainly the only New Democrat present, but the premier had been kind enough to send me an invitation, so I felt obliged to attend.

Nobody spoke to me except a big, tall, slightly balding man in his 40s who made a point of coming over to me and introducing himself. He was Gerald Regan, who, despite political differences, would become a great friend with whom I would spend considerable time over the years, and know well enough to be sure that most, if not all, of the scurrilous things which were said about him were grossly untrue and unfair.

~

One event which occupied much of my time and attention was the notorious, seven-month fishermen's strike at the Strait of Canso and its acrimonious after-effects. Some 200 trawler men from Canso, Petit de Grat and Mulgrave wanted better pay and safer conditions and recognition of the union they had chosen to represent them, the British Columbia-based United Fishermen and Allied Workers Union.

For some years I had been espousing the cause of fishermen who wished to unionize, but legislation which characterized them as "co-adventurers" forbade it. Now they were demanding the right to unionize. While the establishment—fish companies, government, media, churches, etc.—said they were prepared to concede that point, it insisted that the men join the Canadian Food and Allied Workers Union which was endorsed by the Canadian Labour Congress (headed by Joan's uncle, Donald "The Duke" MacDonald), but considered by many to be little better than a "company" union.

One of the bones of contention, the reason frequently given by the fish companies and government for not acceding to the fishermen's requests, was that the UFAWU was said to be Communist. I got deeply involved in the strike and got to know several of the union's leading figures, notably Tom Parkin, Glenn MacEachern and union president Homer Stevens. Stevens, a Cowichan native, was a self-professed Communist and, while undoubtedly sincere in his desire to get justice for Nova Scotia fishermen, was, I believe, quite content to wreak havoc within the capitalist system and was on the lookout for converts if not subverts. He had a mind like a steel trap and was so cold, calculating and determined that I never felt comfortable in his presence.

I had no time for the Communist Party, but I did think the men were (a) entitled to have a union and (b) to have the union they had freely chosen.

In the end, the strike failed miserably, Homer, Tom and Glenn went back to British Columbia, taking some of the fishermen with them. Others quit trawler work and turned to inshore fishing. Most reluctantly joined the CFAWU.

11: Elected at last

In 1970, Premier Smith called an election for October 13. Across the province, things looked grim for the NDP. While Paul and I were able to find candidates for all the Cape Breton seats, the "Halifaxers" did nothing to encourage people to become candidates on the mainland and, while a few of them put their names on ballots, they did not even nominate in all the Halifax/Dartmouth constituencies. As the campaign got under way we only had candidates in just over half of the 46 ridings.

Worse, we even lost one of those when our candidate in Cape Breton West, Nick Clements, went wildly off the rails.

Joan and I had liked Nick and his wife, Betty, and thought him fairly well balanced, but as the election approached ominous warning signs appeared. On the only TV ad (live) we were able to get for him, he rambled on about being "humble" and having "a gut full of gall", and boasted about having cleaned toilets. He talked wildly about sweeping to office with a huge majority, and was rampaging from door to door like a mad man, drunk and violent. He would not listen to anything I tried to tell him and disappeared into the constituency, making himself unreachable.

I realized that we could not allow him to get on the ballot, so I put people to stand on guard outside the Returning Officers' house with instructions to stop Nick from filing his papers by whatever means necessary. I eventually solved the problem by conspiring with his doctor, J.B. Tompkins, a prominent Liberal who was happy to co-operate because Nick's absence from the ballot would almost certainly elect their candidate Allan Sullivan (it did). He had Nick go to see him at the hospital, then sedated him until the deadline had passed.

Many years later, I met Nick in a Dartmouth grocery store. He told me he had spent some years in prison for attempting to harm Betty by backing his car over her, but, as with almost everything Nick said, I did not know if it was true. I heard he died in Alberta in 2019.

In Glace Bay, I was ready, but not overly optimistic. Layton Fergusson was very popular as an individual and had won last time by more than 2,000 votes against Aitchison,

Premier Smith was running a strong campaign with all the media behind him, and we had no money. I had to persuade eight supporters, whom the Credit Union approved, to go on a note for $1,000. At that time, there was no public reimbursement for election expenses, so we had to repay the loan by passing the hat at meetings and rallies.

An additional disadvantage for me, as in every election, was that my presence at the doors in Glace Bay was limited because I had to appear at campaign events all over the province. Also, we had to deal with corruption, particularly from the Conservatives, as bribery was still widely practised. The going rate for a vote was five dollars and a "mickey" of rum. In Paul's constituency, Cape Breton Nova, incumbent Tory Pinky Gaum was passing out nylons and boxes of chocolates.

On Election Day in Ward One, the Tories actually passed out money and rum in front of me on the steps of the poll, taunting me to do something about it. When I complained to the desk sergeant at the police station, he said, "Grow up, Jerry. If you can't play by the rules, get out of the game."

The campaign was pretty standard for those times. Paul and I concentrated on the length of time the Tories had been in office and how little (in our contention) they had done for Cape Breton. His literature and speeches featured the line *"Fourteen Years of Silence and Neglect"*, while my newspaper ads and leaflets announced: *"Fourteen hard, lean years have come and gone, and the Quiet Man has had his chance."*

Everyone knew what that meant because, while Layton was liked as a decent man, he had been as quiet as a mouse in the Legislature. Once when he was Minister of Labour, Layton travelled to Halifax in the same railroad car as United Mineworkers president, Bill Marsh, who was to make his annual presentation to cabinet. Bill told me that Layton looked through the brief, then said, "I wonder what they'll do."

The Conservative campaign was, in my opinion, very good indeed. It concentrated on Smith's experience and stature. TV ads showed him working at his desk late into the night, as a voice asked, *"Is there anyone you would rather have as your premier, than Nova Scotia's premier Ike Smith?"* Impressive daily radio commercials reported on the previous night's rallies, allegedly attended by immense multitudes, at which the premier announced goodies for all.

By contrast, I found the Liberal campaign far less impressive. They concentrated on so-called "scandals" relative to the troubled Heavy Water Plant just outside my constituency; Clairtone, a failed stereo maker which had been given government money; and a strawberry farm near Digby which had also received Tory largesse. I also seem to recall that their platform was an endless list of accomplishments of previous Liberal governments, including one that 16-years-dead premier Angus L. MacDonald had "paved the roads".

Based on all I had seen and heard, I fully expected the Smith government to be handily returned (so did they!). I was both surprised and pleased that they were not, largely because of the fishermen's strike and because voters had come to see them as generally reactionary and anti-labour.

When the smoke cleared on election night, we learned that I had beaten Layton by a handsome total of 1,527 votes and that Paul had squeaked in by 61 votes. Across the province the results were dismal for the NDP. We upped our provincial vote share by only 1.5%. None of our candidates came in second, and only a few received more than 1,000 votes, Jobson and Devanney being two exceptions. The Liberals had narrowly missed winning the popular vote, but had elected 23 MLAs to the Tories' 21.

There was, of course, much nonsense, including from us, I am ashamed to say, about Paul and me "holding the balance of power", something which was only theoretically and temporarily true due to subsequent events, not least Tory Gordon Tidman's being ejected from his Kings West seat following a controverted petition (he had won by only one vote, cast by the Returning Officer!). More than once Paul embarrassed me by telling people we were the two most powerful men in Nova Scotia! I often wished it had been true.

There are two anecdotes I must relate about the 1970 election. The first is that late on election night, long after the result was known in Cape Breton East, I had a phone call from Murdock Matheson, my ward captain in Ward Five. His message almost gave me a heart attack: He told me that he had the ballot boxes from the ward *on his kitchen table* and bade me "come up and get them!" He opined that, since I had won the election, the ballots belonged to me, so he had removed them from the polls, and *the deputy returning officers had let him do it!*

This was highly improper, if not illegal, and I had visions of court cases, a controverted election, and being kicked out of the Legislature even before I had taken my seat.

Fortunately, my next-door neighbour, Dan MacKenzie, was the Returning Officer for the constituency. I went to him and told him what had happened. I knew he could not have got the job had he not been a strong Tory, so I feared he would call the police and bring in the Chief Returning Officer in Halifax.

But he could not have been more decent or more of a gentleman. "Jerry," he said, "You won fair and square. Let's just go up to

Murdock's house, get the boxes and say nothing to anyone about it."

And that is exactly what we did.

The other anecdote concerns Cape Breton Nova, where Paul had won by a whisker. He was an excellent musician and wrote a song for his campaign which was recorded by Herbie and Wilma Gregory recorded and the party broadcast by a mobile loud speaker system:

> *The people are all for Paul,*
> *The Tories don't have a chance at all.*
> *We're going to vote for Paul*
> *Because he's for the people one and all.*

He augmented the campaign's musical repertoire with another of his own compositions:

> Now Tory was a stupid man, who lived in Whitney Pier,
> He sold his vote Election Day for rum or even beer.
> Tory all the way,
> Tory all the way,
> So blind and crazy, drunk and lazy,
> Tory all the way.

The election in Cape Breton Nova had been hectic, if not chaotic, with bribes being dished out by the hundreds. Also, people were being dragged in from the other side of the overpass (the boundary between Nova and Cape Breton South) and sworn in at the poll so they could vote illegally. This was a practice that I suspected, but for which I had no evidence, both we and the Tories were conducting.

Also, spending on publicity was fiercely competitive: the Tories clearly had more money at their disposal, but Paul's campaign seemed to be holding its own, and I often wondered how.

Much later, my good friend Bill Mozvik told me that one dark night he had driven Paul to a lonely spot near the Coke Ovens on

Curry's Lane, where they had parked and waited. After a while, he said, a large car drew up and flashed its headlights, whereupon a man got out whom Bill identified as Al Graham, later Senator, who was a bigwig in the Liberal Party.

He told me Paul went out to meet Graham and took from him a large bag, which Bill said contained a sizable amount of money in cash.

It made sense for the Liberals to help Paul defeat Pinky Gaum as, had he not done so, the outcome would have been 22 MLAs for each of the major parties, in which case the Lieutenant Governor would likely have asked Smith to form another government.

This story may sound far-fetched, but I trusted Bill implicitly, and know from experience that, for all his positive attributes, Paul was not above a bit of skulduggery if it served his purposes.

~

I had only just been elected to the Legislature when the country was hit with a controversial event of major proportions. Just three days after I knew I was going to be an MLA, Prime Minister Pierre Trudeau invoked the 1914 War Measures Act, which suspended the civil liberties of all Canadians from Vancouver Island to St. Johns. He said he had done it at the behest of Quebec Premier Robert Bourassa because Canada was facing an "apprehended insurrection".

On October 5, eight days prior to our election in Nova Scotia, a British diplomat, James Cross, had been abducted by the *Front de Liberation du Québec*, a small gang of crazy amateur thugs who favoured Quebec's independence from Canada. They had been responsible for robberies and bombings for almost a decade, but Cross's kidnapping was judged to have changed their crime spree into an insurrection.

The day following the invocation of the Act, October 17, 1970, the FLQ murdered Quebec's Labour Minister, Pierre LaPorte.

Over the next few weeks, police conducted over 3,000 searches of houses and stores without warrants (often by smashing down the doors) and arrested, detained, and threw into jail for up to three weeks almost 500 people without charge or access to legal counsel. Of those 500, only 45 were eventually charged and only 19 were found guilty of any crime.

When invoking the War Measures Act came before Parliament, the NDP was the only party to oppose it. Leader Tommy Douglas described it as "using a sledge hammer to crack a nut." I was immensely proud of Tommy, because I strongly agreed with him. There was no evidence of FLQ activity outside Quebec so there was no call to suspend civil rights in the nine other provinces, even if you had evidence that the Quebec government was in imminent danger of being taken over (which it was not).

A more recent invocation of the Emergencies Act (which replaced the War Measures Act) was when a convoy of truckers descended on Ottawa in 2022 to protest restrictions imposed in connection with COVID-19. Trudeau Junior's precipitate action was based on even less evidence than was his father's, but gave him power to seize bank accounts, suspend vehicle insurance and interfere with GoFundMe accounts. The reaction to this by NDP Leader Jagmeet Singh could not have been more different from that of Tommy Douglas, or more wrong,

In the event, some 89% of Canadians supported Pierre Trudeau's actions, so it was by no means popular to be the odd man out in any social or public setting. But some things have to be done, so I mounted the steps of the legislature and with a bull horn denounced the War Measures Act as totalitarian overkill. It was the only time in my life that something I had said made the front page redline of the *Chronicle Herald!*

12: Member of the Legislature

I have described in some detail the sensations and emotions of being a newly elected member in my book *What Have You Done for Me Lately?* (the revised edition is available from Moose House Publications), and there is no feeling quite like it, especially if you know that your own efforts and identity were at least as instrumental as your party label in achieving a successful result. In both 1970 and subsequent elections, I believe that to have been true in my own case, and it was certainly true with Paul MacEwan who was elected nine times and on four different tickets: NDP, Independent, Labour Party and Liberal!

Interviews with the media about whether our intentions were to "keep the Regan government in power" and similar nonsense were heady stuff, but difficult to handle because we had no parliamentary experience and simply did not know how things worked, or got done. In one such interview I was sufficiently unwise (stupid would be a better word) to suggest that the province might have a public auto insurance scheme as a result of our position in the House.

Then, in the mail, came a package addressed to *Jeremy Akerman MLA-Elect*, containing 20 sheets of House of Assembly notepaper and as many envelopes, together with a pass for the Canso Causeway and for the Dominion Atlantic Railway. These items came from the Chief Messenger, a Dickensian character with the improbable name of Major Forbes Thrasher, who had, apparently, once been manager of the Lord Nelson Hotel and was a leading expert in heraldry.

When we got to the Legislature we found his appearance and

manner were every bit as Dickensian as his name. He wore striped trousers and a frock coat and, at the beginning of House sittings, would stand to attention in the doorway and scream at the top of his stentorian voice: *"Opennnn the Gallerieeees!"*, whereupon his equally anachronistically-attired minions would then allow the public to enter.

Shortly after the election, Premier Regan called a short fall session of the Legislature, so we dutifully attended, were sworn in and took our seats.

The few times I had been to the Legislature before, I had usually sat in the gallery to observe proceedings, but once I had been ushered on to the floor of the House to make a presentation relative to the province's handling of the Medicare program which the federal government had announced. The committee, chaired by Colchester MLA Gerald Ritcey, treated me with greater kindness than I anticipated, asking me a series of questions, none of which I answered very well, about my mistaken advocacy of an annual premium to finance the plan. In the event, the government chose not to take my advice and wisely funded the program by way of general revenues. But as I sat at the committee table and looked around the chamber, I knew that this was where I belonged (I feel I still do).

Our seats and desks were the furthest from the Speaker to his left, just inside the main door, next to the Sergeant At Arms—another major, Harold Long, who sleepily lounged in an arm chair. Paul's desk was directly behind mine, which made it difficult to confer, and which proved almost unendurable to my ears because, at least in the early days, he addressed the House as if it were a mass meeting, bellowing and roaring.

To our right sat the 21 Tories, their front bench boasting such luminaries as Gordon Tidman, George Snow, Gerry Ritcey, Ken Jones, Gerald Doucet, Tom MacKeough, and Harvey Veniot, all of whom had been ministers in the previous administration. Across from us sat the Liberal government with the brand-new ministers occupying the front row: Scott McNutt, Benoit Comeau, Allan Sullivan, Garnet Brown, Premier Regan, Peter Nicholson, Leonard Pace,

Ralph Fiske, and Bill Gillis.

The sound of pipes and drums announced the arrival of Victor Oland, the Lieutenant Governor, who, dripping with gold braid, lumbered in to deliver the Speech from the Throne. We looked around and saw that a number of members were in striped pants and frock coats, and all were sporting boutonnieres in their buttonholes, the Liberals red, the Tories blue.

Paul and I felt we were in a parallel universe, so stuffy, formal and alien did all this seem to us. We were even more amazed when, in his reply to the Throne Speech, W.S.K. Jones, acting leader of the opposition (Ike Smith had stepped down as party leader), railed on about the "architectural rape of Province House", referring to Regan's having installed a partition on the lower level near his office. This we found astonishing in light of our belief that unemployment, workers compensation and health care were infinitely more pressing matters.

The overall impression we gained was of a Victorian charade; although I confess that, as time went on, I came to rather like the pomp and ceremony and think that, at least, it does no harm.

Another feature of the Legislature in 1970 which surprised us was the louche if not licentious atmosphere which prevailed in the building once the House had risen for the day, which seemed in dramatic contrast to the stiff formality of the proceedings on the floor. It was well known that, up in the Hansard Office, which recorded and printed the proceedings of each session, MLAs and staff were fraternizing in a more than platonic way (after the 1974 election Buddy MacEachern and Walter Fitzgerald were frequent visitors); that the Sergeant At Arms, Major Long, regularly invited page girls back to parties in his trailer at night; and that some MLAs made free with the facilities in ways for which they were never intended.

Once, when I went back to the darkened chamber to get some papers from my desk, I heard unmistakable sounds coming behind the Speaker's chair. I stealthily crept forward and took a peek. There was Raymond Smith, MLA for Cumberland Center, *in flag-*

rante delicto with one of the female staff.

The limit to my own after-hours participation was going to the premier's office, where as many as a dozen people might be lounging around guzzling Scotch and smoking huge cigars. Scott McNutt, Garnet Brown and Allan Sullivan were regulars, as were Regan's staff members David Thompson and Mike Kirby, and some members of the media, foremost among them the loquacious Doug Harkness.

~

During my overly-lengthy maiden speech, the recording equipment broke down so that, mercifully, posterity has been denied a complete written record of it. I talked a lot about coal miners and widows who then received a pitiful pension. Regan was most complimentary and the Liberals applauded.

The Conservatives were hostile towards us and treated us as interlopers, although in time I became great friends with some of them. Of course, one reason why the government members were nice to us was that, although we did not strictly hold the balance of power, some votes would be very close.

The Speaker, George Mitchell (a marvellous gentleman and a scrupulously fair chairman), only voted in the event of a tie so, if one or two MLAs were absent or sick, government measures could be lost. A few resolutions and bills which I introduced actually passed Second Reading because George (quite properly) voted for them so as to "allow further consideration".

Soon, we learned the ropes and knew the rules inside out and how to take advantage of them. In those days, MLAs were allowed to speak for a whole hour on any motion or bill, and we very frequently used (or maybe I should say abused) that right. Also Question Period then had no time limit, and often we would take it well into the evening. Ten years later, I chaired a committee of Arthur Donahoe and Hugh Tinkham which completely revised the Rules of the House and put a stop to the practices in which I had once revelled.

Contrary to popular belief, being an MLA in 1970 was by no means a lucrative occupation. Today, MLAs get about $90,000 a year (much more if they are Ministers, Speaker, Deputy Speaker, whips, house leaders or committee chairs), many funded trips between Halifax and their constituencies, living expenses in Halifax for hotels/apartments and meals, office and staff in the constituency, and other benefits. Back then, we received a grand total of $7,500 a year plus free postage from Province House. Any meals, travel and hotel costs had to come out of the one payment which we received once a year in a lump.

It was almost impossible to survive on the money, so we were always looking for bargains. This leads me to my weird and amusing association with one of the Conservative MLAs.

I have the impression that the atmosphere in today's House of Assembly would not permit the kind of cross-party friendships which were possible in my time as an MLA. I enjoyed a number of such friendships, particularly with Tories Gerald Doucet, Harry How and George Snow; and Liberals Gerald Regan, Allan Sullivan and Peter Nicholson. The one of which I relate here was with a colourful character known to most as Harvey A.

Prior to his entering politics, Harvey Veniot had been a lawyer in Pictou County. He was famous, among other things, for flattering judges in order to make them more favourably disposed to his clients. He used to compliment a judge for even mundane utterances, saying he thought "more of your lordship's dicta should be published so others might learn from the wisdom." The judges knew what he was up to, but played along. As Harvey told me: "Never did any harm to try it on, and maybe it worked once or twice."

By the time I got to the Legislature, Harvey had been there for 14 years representing Pictou West, had been Speaker and for some years Minister of Municipal Affairs and Minister of Agriculture. One day, he came and sat by my desk as the other members were filing out of the chamber and told me that I reminded him of himself when he was young. He told me he had always been a vigorous reformer and intimated—without actually saying so—that he had more than once been tempted to leave the Tories and join the NDP.

I did not believe a word of it and, seeing this on my face, Harvey laughed heartily. Harvey said he had heard that the annual indemnity was my only income and that I should "tag along" with him to "learn some tricks of the trade." When he learned I was staying at the Carlton on Argyle Street he expressed horrified amazement. "Waste of good money, boy! You gotta understand that if you're going to spend money at all, spend it in your constituency where it will buy you votes. Every cent you spend in Halifax is money down the toilet!"

He told me had found a place, owned by "good Pictou County people", where he could get me a room for $15. I told him that wouldn't be any help because I was already paying $12 a night. "No boy!' Harvey cried, digging me in the ribs, "not a night! $15 a week, boy!" I agreed with alacrity.

The place, on South Street, was grim. It was obvious we would be getting what we paid for. The good Pictou County people clearly believed as little in spending money as Harvey did. My tiny room had a window which let in the air and rain, a rickety bed with springs sticking through the mattress, plaster falling from the ceiling and wallpaper peeling in long, damp spirals.

When I asked to see Harvey's room, he hesitated, then explained with some embarrassment that he only paid $11 a week for his accommodation because of who he was, adding: "These people look up to me."

Harvey was installed in a dirty, dusty room that was totally bare save for a strip of burlap stretched across one corner. Behind the burlap was Harvey's "room": a palette made of old newspapers and two threadbare blankets. "No point in throwing good money away on fancy hotels," Harvey said emphatically.

The morning after my first night chez good Pictou County people, Harvey and I strode up Barrington Street towards the Legislature. There was a department store (Woolworth's, I think) which had a lunch counter with tall bar stools. They advertised breakfast, so when we got there I turned into the store.

Harvey grabbed my arm, furiously pulling me back into the

street, crying "No, no! Early bird! Early bird! Monday!"

Rather alarmed, I asked Harvey what he meant.

He explained that bacon and eggs at the lunch counter were much too expensive except on Mondays, when they ran an "Early Bird Special" for a dollar. "We only go there on Mondays," Harvey said severely, "for the Early Bird. Rest of the week we'll have to get by with toast and a muffin."

Reluctantly, I gave in and docilely followed to him to Denlock's Acadian Grill, across from the Legislature, which a nice man called Spiros then operated. Having ordered our toast and muffin I asked Spiros for coffee, whereupon Harvey became quite agitated and barked: "Cancel that, Spiros! Cancel the coffee!"

He grabbed the food and hustled me out on to the sidewalk. "You're not thinking, boy," Harvey said, sadly shaking his head. "We can get free coffee over at the House of Assembly. Why pay for it here when you can get it for nothing?"

I thought I had seen the limits of Harvey's tight-fistedness, until one morning when we were walking up Barrington Street and Harvey pointed to a second-hand store, long since demolished. "Come on in, boy," he said. "They have a great deal on used razor blades."

I could not believe my ears, but, sure enough, for pennies Harvey bought a bundle of clearly used blades and carefully doled out two into my hand. "I won't charge you for those," he said. "Of course you can't get too many shaves out of them, but you can get three or four if you go easy."

It was rumoured that Harvey was fairly well off, owned rental property and had a good stock portfolio. Once we were debating a bill affecting a large company which did business in the province. Harvey got into the debate, sternly arguing that provisions of the legislation were unfair to the company.

Ike Smith then jumped up and announced that he had to "declare an interest" because he owned some stock in the company. Red-faced, Harvey sheepishly pulled himself to his feet again, and quietly confessed that he too owned "one or two shares".

Later, in the lobby, I asked Ike if he knew how many shares Harvey did own. "More than I do," said Ike dryly.

Sometime after the Liberal government had passed legislation to set up an Ombudsman for the province, Premier Regan rose in the House and invited John Buchanan and me to go down to his office and help him select a person to fill the position. Jerry and John went ahead of me because I had a quick question to ask in the chamber.

Just as I was about to go into the premier's office I heard a loud "Pssssst!" I look around and saw Harvey lurking behind the stairs. He pulled me over and said he would like me to put his name forward for Ombudsman. "I know John can't afford to lose me from the caucus, but he knows I'll do a good job."

Since I genuinely thought Harvey could do the job well, I promised I would advance his name in the meeting. When I did so a few minutes later, both Regan and Buchanan burst into laughter. When I told John what Harvey had said, their laughter became even louder.

I still think Harvey would have been better than the successful applicant, a man who subsequently got into trouble for using his office to attack me and had to be reprimanded by the Speaker of the House.

Harvey left politics in 1974 and Premier Buchanan later appointed him a judge. I never observed his court, but I am told he dispensed justice with fairness and dignity. He died in 2009, aged 93.

~

In that first term I also made friends with Regan's right hand man, the remarkable Peter Nicholson, Minister of Finance and Education; and with Gerry Doucet, the Conservative MLA for Richmond. Always generous, Peter would invite me to dinner at The Gondola on South Street, or to the apartment which he his wife rented in the building into which I later moved and where I have lived for more than thirty years.

Gerry and I sometimes vacationed together and played golf, a game I liked but at which I was terribly inept. I will have more to say about Peter and Gerry later, as indeed I will about many of the people I knew during those years. Each will have an entry in a sort of "Rogues' Gallery" which you will find towards the end of this book.

But Gerald Regan was a friend of a different kind, and I keenly miss him and resent his no longer being on this earth. He would call me late at night, asking my advice on what the government should do about this or that and, acutely embarrassing to me, would criticize or make fun of a number of his cabinet ministers and caucus members, to whom he had given nicknames.

Not surprisingly, Peter Nicholson (Annapolis West) was "Nikol", Jack Hawkins (Hants East) was "The Hawk", Fraser Mooney (Yarmouth) "Moon" and Harold Huskilson (Shelburne) "The Husk"; but less complimentarily, Glenn Bagnell (Dartmouth North) was "The Sneak", Walton Cook (Lunenburg Centre) was "The Lunatic", and poor Bill Gillis (Antigonish) was "The Death of the Virgin".

His nickname for himself was "Preem". Unsurprisingly, Gerry Doucet was "Douce", and I was "Ake".

Then he would tell me what happened in cabinet and who had said what. When I would tell him that I did not *want* to be in possession of such information, he would say: "But Ake, you're the only one I can trust."

I responded that he should *not* trust me because I might inadvertently use in a speech something he had told me in confidence. In any event, I said, it circumscribed my work, even though engaging in personalities rather than discussing policy was never part of my style.

The premier had arranged to let Paul and me have a tiny room in the basement next to the toilet. One day, when I was exploring in the vicinity, I found an unmarked door which opened onto a vast, very low-ceilinged, dark, dusty, underground cavern full of ancient furniture and boxes of books and papers.

At one location there was a sort of hole in the ceiling into which a person could stand upright. I did this, only to discover that I was directly under the floor boards of the cabinet room and that every word said above was audible. I listened and took notes.

That night, when Jerry called me, I told him that he did not need to tell me what happened in cabinet that day because *I* would tell *him*. He was astounded and agitated, demanding to know who my informant was, but I could not keep him in suspense for long and revealed my secret.

When I went there again after the weekend, the space had been filled in with concrete and a metal plate!

~

The 50th General assembly ground on for four years, during which time the government enacted various reforms, our having aggressively tried to keep them on their toes. There was no measure of any kind on which either Paul or I did not speak—whether or not we knew what we were talking about, as frequently we didn't!

Of the people in Hansard told me that I had done more talking, and taken up more space in Hansard, in the time I had been in the House than any other MLA in history. One headline in a national publication was particularly gratifying, if undoubtedly exaggerated: *Two man NDP team shows heels to Tories.*

During that period, the Conservatives chose a new leader in John Buchanan, who had sat next to me in the House after Gordon Tidman had been ejected. My friend Gerry Doucet had led on the first ballot, but Buchanan had won the next one as a result of Dartmouth Mayor Roland Thornhill throwing his support to John.

Gerry was very bitter, alleging that religious prejudice (he was Catholic) and other shenanigans had been at work. He rapidly lost interest in politics, and announced he would not re-offer in the next election.

In any event, Gerry had other interests to distract him, namely a clandestine affair with a married woman whom he later married and with whom he was blissfully happy. On at least one occasion, he had me act as a go-between, delivering a message (or maybe a package) to Vida, who was living at Whidden's trailer park in Antigonish while her divorce was in progress.

When Buchanan became leader, naturally he moved his seat to the centre position on the Tory front bench, so I had now had George Snow from Yarmouth as my right hand next door neighbour. George was a fisherman, and a very brave one, having been instrumental in the rescue of the crew of the shipwrecked *Nelson B.* in 1967. He was down to earth and no nonsense, but was kindly and had an impish sense of humour.

We became good friends and, whenever I could, I would visit him and his English wife, Marjorie, at their home in Port Maitland. Sadly, George left us in 2020 at the age of 97.

Others I got to know and like of the 1970 intake were Jim MacLean, Garnet Brown and Harry How. Later, in subsequent Assemblies, I also became friends with Rollie Thornhill who had, as it were, deprived Gerry Doucet of the Conservative leadership. Jim MacLean was aggressive, acerbic and personal in debate, but friendly and generous in private. Jim would spend hours in the Legislative Library looking for quips and insults he could use in speeches. Some were wickedly good, others childish, such as his remark to Scott MacNutt: "Why doesn't the minister be like his head and come to a point?"

When my parents visited me and I drove them around the Cabot Trail, Jim and his wife Toby, treated them as if they were royalty.

~

One interesting event during that period was a dinner the province held at the Savoy Hotel in London to promote industrial development and tourism, at which Princess Anne and Captain Phillips were the guests of honour (I say more about this event when I discuss Gerald Regan in detail in the "Rogues' Gallery"). The premier had asked John Buchanan and me to go, and to each host a table of prominent persons.

My table had a mixture of bankers, developers and scientists, but was dominated by multi-millionaire newspaper mogul, Lord Thomson of Fleet. His lordship declined the rich, fancy dishes the

Savoy's chefs had prepared, instead ordering a plain omelette.

When the Havana cigars were passed round with the Cognac and coffee, he took a huge handful and stuffed them into his pocket. Leaning close to me he said, "I don't smoke. These are for my chauffeur."

When I told him I was from Cape Breton, he immediately said, "Ah, the *Cape Breton Post*! One of mine."

I asked him how many newspapers he owned. At this distance I cannot be precise, but I think he said he had 253. The conversation then went as follows:

"Will you buy more newspapers?"

"Yes, of course."

"Why do you want to buy more newspapers?"

"So I can make more money."

"Why do you want to make more money?"

"So I can buy more newspapers."

~

I must mention one other event which occurred during out first term in the Legislature. It was announced by the Chronicle Herald's quaintly anachronistic headline: FISTICUFFS ERUPT IN HOUSE.

This was the co-called MacEwan-Laffin affair, about which everyone and his brother has their own version, which they swear is the true account. Not long ago, I listened to a former Tory Leader stand not ten feet away from me and tell a version of this incident which bore no relation to fact. I know because I was there; he was not.

News media, commentators including Edmund Morris, cartoonists like Bob Chambers, and those with ulterior motives all disseminated misinformation. Even some who were in the chamber at the time got it wrong, whether or not intentionally. I was closest to the action, uncomfortably close, so I am entitled to ask readers to accept no version other than my own.

To understand the incident some little background is required.

Tory Mike Laffin (Cape Breton Centre), a dentist, and Paul MacEwan (Cape Breton Nova) had contiguous constituencies and had developed a bitter rivalry. A measure of this sentiment could be seen in a song Paul wrote and widely distributed, which commenced with:

> *Why was Laffin laughin'*
> *When his horse he was a-trottin',*
> *Why was Laffin laughin'*
> *When our teeth they were a-rottin'?*

The town of New Waterford, in Laffin's riding, derived its water supply from Waterford Lake which was located over the boundary in Paul's riding. The only other background you need to know is that, at the time, Mike's brother John was assistant to the President of the Nova Scotia Power Commission (later Corporation) which owned the lake.

For reasons which were then as now irrelevant, the water supply was not as pure and clean as usual and, not unnaturally, residents were concerned. Laffin raised the matter in Question Period, foolishly saying that because the lake was in Paul's constituency, he was to blame for the problem.

Outraged, Paul immediately jumped to his feet and retorted, equally foolishly, that since the Power Commission owned the lake, it was Laffin's brother who was to blame.

Laffin left his desk and came charging down the aisle. For the first split second I thought he was going to stomp out of the chamber. In the second split second it looked as if he were coming for me.

Just before he drew level with me, and as I heard Paul jump up behind me, Laffin started his swing—I felt the wind from it. Passing my ear, it landed in Paul's face.

It was all over by the time the Sergeant At Arms, lazy as ever, had lumbered to his feet. Liberal Ron Wallace, a former boxer, darted into the aisle but was also too late.

Paul stood there bleeding as the Speaker George Mitchell "named" Laffin and suspended him "from the services of the House".

In the Committee on Rules and Privileges, chaired by the premier, much was made of Mike's having been a prisoner of war, and he was given a rap on the knuckles. I think it was suspension for a week, or maybe two.

Since Paul MacEwan had never been popular with the media (nor they with him!) many said that Paul had "started it". Tories and others said that Paul had "squared off" as if that justified Laffin's attack.

Laffin went home to a hero's welcome in New Waterford, and we swore that come the next election we would take him out (we did).

In light of events in the House many years later involving Percy Paris and Keith Colwell, it is worth mentioning that at no time did Paul and I contemplate bringing in the police. Had we done so, the valuable collegiality which then existed in the Legislature would have vanished overnight. It was a House matter and the House dealt with it.

What is known to very few is that, not too long after that incident, Laffin assaulted me in the lobby just outside the chamber.

There had been a terrible, fatal accident at Number 12 Colliery in New Waterford and I had asked about it in Question Period. Mike was enraged, quite wrongly believing that I had no business asking about his constituency, so he grabbed me and shoved me against the wall, pressing me with his body and snarling in my face.

I pushed him away, walked back into the chamber and said no more about it.

Strangely, but happily to relate, as time marched on both Paul and I became friends with Mike. He even took Paul up in his plane, and to harness racing events in which Mike competed.

~

I don't intend to relate the proceedings of the House of Assembly in detail, listing the bills and resolutions passed and budgets presented. All that, including what everybody said, is all in the public record for those who are interested. Rather, here I am trying to convey my impressions of the place at the time, and to tell anecdotes which I think are interesting or amusing, or possibly both.

Suffice it to say that my first term in the House saw the controversial legislation to take Nova Scotia Light and Power under public ownership, which we supported (the Tories opposed it), and the so-called Michelin Bill, the terms of which, contrary to the expectations of Regan, a labour lawyer, were restrictive and which we characterized as "anti-labour" and dictated by the French company.

Ironically, since the Tories had not been overly accommodating to labour, Ike Smith, as combative as ever, joined me in a lengthy fight against this legislation, and we worked as a team trying to undermine the bill. Ike and I also sat on the Law Amendments Committee where, to the annoyance and frustration of other members —especially chairman Len Pace—we conducted lofty and lengthy ideological debates, he asserting that capital drove the economy, I that without labour nothing could be produced.

Ike was out of action for some time, having had a heart attack, and did not re-offer in the next election. He was an extremely able and honourable man who had been a Member of the Legislature for 25 years and had given outstanding service to the province.

Although a few clung on, most of the anti-Akerman elements within the NDP faded away as the 50th Assembly progressed, and fairly sensible, reliable people (or so I thought at the time) replaced them. It was not until later in the decade that a new, more vicious, more ideologically motivated opposition sprang up, whose activities led to my resignation from both Legislature and party.

In 1972 there was a federal election in which Conservative MP Donald MacInnis ran again in Cape Breton East Richmond. Our candidate was Reserve Mines county councillor Jake Currie, a thoroughly decent man, who improved upon the vote I had obtained in 1968, but was still 2,000 short. His was one of many campaigns I would manage over the ensuing years.

In the neighbouring constituency, incumbent Robert Muir won in a landslide with 15,394, our candidate, Bill Mozvik, receiving 7,134 votes. Clearly, this composition of Paul's had little effect on the outcome:

> *Way down in a horse barn,*
> *All filled with manure,*
> *I heard a mare whinny:*
> *"Don't vote for Bob Muir."*

~

When I was an MLA, the most frequent calls upon my time were claims before the Workmen's Compensation Board (as it was then called). Workmen's Compensation was established in Nova Scotia as early as 1917, but not primarily for workers, as one might imagine, but to protect employers from lawsuits arising from the many injuries and deaths sustained, primarily in the province's coal mines (which at that time provided the bulk of provincial revenues) and at the Trenton and Sydney steel works. It was therefore compulsory for both workers and employers: Workers would (in theory) be compensated for injury or death and it would not be legal for the company to be sued.

The Board operated according to what was known as the "Meat Chart", which illustrated various body parts and how much money would be awarded for the loss of each. This was a Victorian symbol of an antediluvian attitude which seldom if ever accounted for the total effect on the worker and his ability to continue to be employed. For conditions which were not obvious on the surface, the decision on whether compensation would be awarded was at the discretion of the medical personnel.

Thus it was that, while then-Chairman and former Tory MLA for Cumberland Centre Stephen Pyke was an amenable, friendly fellow, he always took the position that the Medical Director, Dr. Dobson had the last word.

I never met Dr. Dobson, but he seemed to me to be the embodiment of callousness, and contempt for the working man, especially in cases involving pulmonary function. Since, in those days, almost all miners smoked cigarettes, Dr. Dobson dismissed most claims they might make of loss of lung function as having been caused not by black lung, but by their smoking habits.

This struck me as being unfair, so I got in touch with a Dr. Rasmussen in West Virginia, who had been conducting experiments on coal miners involving a form of magnetometry, in which the miner was placed before a massive fan which aligned the particles of silica and allowed them to be recorded. I then contacted a Dr. Gerhard Stronick at Dalhousie University, who kindly set up the necessary equipment, before which I paraded a succession of Cape Breton coal miners whom I drove in batches to Halifax. The results were startling, but Dr. Dobson fought us every inch of the way.

At that point, in 1973, I established the Automatic Assumption Society and asked District 26 United Mineworkers International Board Member Jack Delaney to be president, myself serving as secretary. The name suggests what we were all about: It was that any miner who had more than twenty years in the pit and had appreciable loss of lung function had to be *assumed* to have acquired the condition at least in part to his working environment.

On this principle, and with the help of Dr. Stronick's findings, we vigorously lobbied government. After years of hard work and many affected miners having passed away, automatic assumption eventually became law.

13: More elections

In late February, 1974 the premier called an election to be held on April 2. I think we were expecting the House to be called into session, but instead got this nasty surprise.

For the first time in history the NDP had candidates in every constituency, one of those candidates being my current wife's father, Frank Boone. In light of our having run many more candidates than in 1970, our upping our vote by 6.3% to 13% was not as great an achievement as it at first seemed. But it gave every Nova Scotia adult the opportunity to vote for us.

Unfortunately, only 56,000 of them chose to do so, to the Tories' 166,000 and the winning Liberals' 206,000. Regan's government was returned to office with an increase of eight seats, one of them Pictou West, where my old chum Harvey Veniot lost by 22 votes. The Conservatives lost nine seats.

We picked up one seat, fulfilling our vow to defeat Mike Laffin in Cape Breton Centre, where our candidate, James "Buddy" MacEachern won by 637 votes. Paul's majority climbed to 1475, and mine jumped to a whopping 2,475.

Also encouraging was that in Cape Breton North, Len Arsenault received a very respectable 3,300 votes, marking that constituency as our Number One target the next time. Caroll Anne's dad also did quite well, racking up 2,269.

Three new inductees into the Legislature were of particular interest: In Dartmouth South, Roland Thornhill beat Scott MacNutt, and was to sit in the House for close to 20 years, most of it as a senior cabinet minister. Thornhill, a handsome Newfoundlander with a rich bass voice, was a fine orator and an extremely skilful politician who, in time, became a special friend.

In Pictou East, a feisty, combative, rather spiteful young farmer, Donald Cameron, was elected for the Tories. Much later, he became premier, but in the interim was a participant in some questionably seedy activities, of which more below.

In Colchester, Melinda MacLean was elected for the Liberals, being the second woman in history to sit in the Legislature. She was intelligent, able, well spoken, good looking, but was never appointed to the cabinet. When I asked Regan why, he cryptically replied, "She has blotted her copybook," but would not elaborate.

Subsequently, I learned Melinda was having a torrid affair with Attorney General Allan "Sully" Sullivan, and it was typical of the times that when both were thought to be behaving badly, it was the female who was punished. Even after Sully resigned in 1976 to become a judge, Melinda was not elevated. This was atypical and unworthy of Regan, and I told him so.

~

The most significant events during the course of the 51st Assembly from my point of view were the birth of my son, Gareth, on April 10th, my becoming ill with pericarditis, and the notorious so-called "page girl affair".

My getting pericarditis gave me additional insight into the lives of many of the miners I served. One of the most frequent types of accident in a coal mine involves the back, and over the years hundreds of miners were sent to Halifax to receive a myelogram, prior to a possible spinal fusion.

A myelogram is a diagnostic imaging test using contrasting dye and X-rays to discover possible problems in the spine. A needle is inserted into the spinal canal (lumbar puncture) and a certain amount of spinal fluid is removed and replaced by the dye. The patient is then put on a floating platform and, as the platform tilts the dye travels down the spine and around the brain, the X-ray machine showing where the passage of the dye reveals any obstructions.

The problem is that the amount of fluid inserted into the spinal canal has to be exactly the same as the fluid taken out, otherwise extraordinary pressures are brought to bear in the head, causing massive pain. This happened to me and, when it did, I finally understood why so many miners had described the procedure as 'hell on earth'.

Originally the doctors had thought my problem was not the heart but the spine, and this is why they gave me the myelogram. They were mistaken, but for weeks, I could not raise myself from a lying position without the pain surging to my head, accompanied by violent vomiting.

As long as I could lie in bed in the old Halifax Infirmary, things were not too bad, as my assistant Marty Dolin brought (and fed me) various tempting dishes from the Five Fishermen restaurant, and I received first-class attention from Dr. Arthur Shears (a Glace Bay native) and a Yugoslavian nurse. But my nominating meeting for the next election was due in Glace Bay in a matter of days and I could hardly be nominated *in absentia*.

So I got a young man to drive me home while I lay flat on the back seat. Some five and a half hours later, at the Firemen's Parlours in Glace Bay I half sat/half lay in the meeting with my head on the table, and when it came time to give my acceptance speech I managed to get out three sentences before rushing to the washroom to throw up.

The meeting was clearly aghast, but when I explained why I was behaving so oddly, there were nods in the crowd from miners who had been through the same experience. If not exactly one of them, I was at last a kindred spirit.

A friend in Bermuda, David Wilkinson, MP, invited me to go to his estate to recuperate. I had my own cottage not far from the astonishingly-blue water's edge and gradually healed in the sun.

While I was there I met a variety of Bermudian politicians, on both sides of the aisle, and became deeply involved in a plot to oust the premier, Jack Sharpe, whom my friends thought too dull and prosaic to win the next election. The plotters included David, a rambunctious MP of Portuguese origin, Harry Viera, and senators

John Stubbs and Stan Rattray. It was fun to attend the meetings at which we discussed various schemes and in which I participated freely with the luxury of knowing that I had nothing to lose regardless of the outcome.

That outcome was that we had garnered enough of the United Bermuda Party MPs to force Sharpe to step down, which he duly did. Our man, David Gibbons, replaced him and served as premier for four years.

Just as with the Laffin-MacEwan fisticuffs affair, the so-called "Page Girl Affair" is an instance where everybody "knows" what happened, but if you press them, you will find that they heard it from someone who heard it from someone else who had it "on good authority".

On my return from Bermuda, now in restored health and vigour, I went to the Legislature. As I was going up the Granville Street steps, an out-of-town journalist, I think from the *Globe and Mail*, accosted me. He asked me for my reaction to the allegation that the premier had sexually assaulted, maybe even raped, one of the page girls.

His story was as lurid as something out the *National Enquirer*, the gruesome details of which, according to him, were that Regan had lured the young woman into his office, had taken out his penis and said, "Here it is. I know you want it. Take it." He told me that Harold Long, the Sergeant at Arms, had heard the words from the outer office.

I was immediately skeptical because Long was a seamy character with a bitter grudge against the premier for not having given him a prominent position in the receiving line for the Queen's visit the previous year. I was also suspicious because I knew the premier's office door was heavily padded and that you could barely hear voices inside even if they were shouting.

I brushed off the journalist, truthfully telling him that this was the first I had heard of the matter, and went straight down to the premier's office. His secretary, Joan Shoveller, said she had been waiting for me to come, that the premier was out of town but had said that as soon as I arrived I should go to see Peter Nicholson.

Peter was one of the most honest, decent and upright men I have ever known, so I believe that what he told me was the truth, or at very least what he firmly believed to be true. He said that, as soon as he had got wind of the allegation, he had called in Halifax CID and asked them to investigate. They did so, and reported that the whole thing was a fabrication concocted by Harold Long and Donald Cameron. Peter said he had told the police not to pursue any kind of charges because it would only make matters worse and turn a tempest in a teapot into a full-fledged hurricane.

This was not the only time Cameron tried to frame Gerald Regan. My wife, who was then working in the NDP caucus office, told me that, on several occasions, Cameron and Buddy MacEachern tried to persuade her to go to Regan's office, flirt with him and entice him into a compromising position. They told her not to worry because "someone" would be nearby if she needed help, but she emphatically refused to have anything to do with such sordid entrapment.

It did not surprise me to hear this about Cameron, but that one of my own caucus members would engage in such behaviour still sickens me.

~

Hot on the heels of the provincial election in 1974, the Liberal government in Ottawa was defeated on its budget in May, precipitating a federal election. I was determined to defeat Donald MacInnis, who, though undoubtedly sincere, had been misleading retired coal miners into believing that they were entitled to, and would receive, millions of dollars from the Cape Breton Development Corporation.

When Donald had first raised the matter, I was somewhat skeptical but hoped he was right because the miners deserved everything they could get. I went to see Tom Kent, who was president of DEVCO, and tackled him on the subject.

He was so indignant and furious about the clamour Donald had raised, that I could tell that his stubbornness would never permit him to give in, no matter how much pressure was applied. As a result, the years went by and the money was not forthcoming, though, naturally, many retired miners did not want to hear this and clung to the hope.

In his customary fashion, Paul wrote a song, which went like this:

> *I just went out New Waterford way,*
> *Took a little trip around Glace Bay,*
> *All the folks they shout out "Hey,*
> *Donald, where's the money?"*

I racked my brains to think of a candidate who could defeat such a formidable opponent. One day, I happened to see Joe Hogan on the street, and an audacious notion entered my head.

Joe's brother, Andrew, was a Catholic priest who had gained fame and a large following from a TV series called *The People's School*, which had aired for some years. I asked Joe what his brother had been doing since the series ended, and he told me Andy was teaching at St. Francis Xavier University in Antigonish.

Shortly afterwards, when Grace McInnis (daughter of J.S. Woodsworth), the MP for Vancouver-Kingsway, was visiting Cape Breton, I roped her into taking a drive with me to the university. There we saw Hogan and asked him to be our candidate.

He was immediately interested and said that if his bishop would consent, he was up for it. A few days later he called me and told me that all systems were go, so I leaked it to the media.

The reaction was satisfying: it seemed everybody was talking about Hogan coming home to Cape Breton to run for parliament, and almost everyone I heard from greeted the idea positively, if not enthusiastically.

In short order, Donald MacInnis announced that he would not be re-offering as the Conservative candidate. I do not know if Donald's decision was prompted by Hogan's entry into the fray, but I believe that if they had squared off, Hogan still would have won, but not nearly by the margin he actually achieved.

I nominated Hogan at a jam-packed convention at the LOC Hall in Dominion. At the meeting, Blaise MacDonald, lawyer son of the Tory Mayor of Glace Bay, Dan Alec MacDonald, approached me and offered his services.

Together, Blaise and I ran a rip-roaring campaign, including a motorcade which stretched from New Aberdeen in Glace Bay to the New Waterford town boundary, almost 14 kilometres. The motorcade had various floats on which a variety of musical performers played, but it lacked the one thing on which Blaise had set his heart: He had desperately wanted an elephant and made numerous calls to that end, but, alas, was unsuccessful.

As expected, Paul MacEwan produced a campaign song:

> *Are you for Hogan, for Andy Hogan?*
> *The folks from Framboise, Louisbourg, Reserve,*
> *Are all for Hogan, for Andy Hogan,*
> *And victory they richly deserve.*
> *In Glace Bay and Dominion and New Waterford,*
> *The folks are all a-shouting: "Hogan. All aboard!"*
> *Are you for Hogan, for Andy Hogan,*
> *The man who stands by you!*

Hogan was elected with a majority of 4,464 over the Liberal, the Tories coming third. Paul, Buddy and I were jubilant, but if we thought having Hogan as an MP would make our lives easier we were in for a rude awakening.

Over the six years he was an MP, we found Andy to be an arrogant, cranky, pompous individual who would lecture us on how to do our work and conduct politics, but was slack on his own duties and played only a minor role in party activities. Most of the time we could not even get him to make financial contributions to his own association.

Worse, though all three of us had our plates more than full with our MLA work, Andy shuffled off federal paperwork to us, and referred constituents to us whom he should have assisted himself. Friends in the federal caucus told me that in Ottawa, Andy was not diligent, attentive, or willing to learn the ropes, and was unhappy he was not treated as one of the stars of the caucus.

Buddy MacEachern christened him *The Priestly Prick* and many times this seemed more than appropriate.

~

Over the next four years, a new, major issue arose within the province as electricity prices soared due to the so-called "energy crisis" and the government's inability to continue to heavily subsidize the Nova Scotia Power Corporation. This was a problem which nobody could solve, and for which none of the parties had a solution, although the Conservatives naturally lambasted Regan, blaming him for events occurring around the world.

In mid-August 1978, Regan finally called an election for September 19. We all knew that power rates would be an instrumental factor, but just how decisive was yet to be determined.

On Election Day, we found out. It transpired that the Regan government had been booted out, dropping from 31 seats to 17. John Buchanan's Tories jumped from 12 to 31, and we picked up one, Cape Breton North, which Len Arsenault won by 663 votes.

Paul's majority was 1,051, Buddy's 601, and mine had dropped to 1,953, largely due to an excellent Tory candidate, Frank Edwards (later a judge), whom, until the moment he announced, I had been led to believe by Blaise MacDonald would be supporting, and working, for me.

Our popular vote crept up to 14.4%, for which we spent a total $38,873. The Tories spent $274,623, and the Liberals $390,554.

As expected, Roland Thornhill received a major portfolio, Development. He expected to get Finance, but I had told him at dinner a few days before that I was sure the new premier would keep that for himself, and so it turned out.

I believe John did it that way so he could start large borrowings (the total of which later became massive) and that that was why, when he eventually did personally relinquish the portfolio, he for the most part appointed ministers who were not as independent-minded as Rollie, and would invariably, if not always, defer to him on numerous new bond issues John would need in order to appease various interest groups looking for money. I am just as sure that John knew that if he gave Finance to Rollie, he would meet with resistance,, and I am equally sure that, had Rollie got the job, Nova Scotia would not have accumulated the enormous debt it did during the Buchanan years.

The 1978 election intake included some interesting and/or remarkable individuals who had been elected on the Conservative ticket. Ken Streatch, a fine gentleman; Tom McInnis (later a Senator), one of my very few defenders within the cabinet; Ron Russell, a feisty little New Zealander who became Speaker; Rev. Laird Stirling of whom John later appointed me "watchdog"; and the able, urbane and exceptionally likeable Donahoe brothers, Terry and Arthur, of whom I shall have much more to say later on in the "Rogue's Gallery".

~

During this period, the NDP had for some months the services of Ted Chudyk, who was a fundraiser for the Manitoba NDP, where Ed Schreyer was the premier. I had spent years believing, and saying, that whilst the "old line parties" were corrupt and in debt to "big business", the NDP was as pure as the driven snow, being funded only by the nickels and dimes of "ordinary people". Chudyk was a revelation.

He had been a professional gambler and boasted of owning a white silk suit. He explained to me how the Manitoba NDP raised money from the liquor companies. Frank Syms, from Reserve Mines but then Treasurer of the Manitoba NDP, later confirmed what Chudyk had told me.

Ted told me that when he went to see the companies' CEOs (usually in Toronto or Montreal) he not only told them that they had to make a political contribution in order to sell products through the Manitoba Liquor Corporation, but they had to pay a fee to the NDP for each product listed, and an additional fee for each product placed on shelves which were at the eye-line level.

This was just one of a large number of factors leading to my eventual disillusionment. Another large one was that I was becoming increasingly aware that I was advocating policies which either could not be afforded or would not work, and was essentially telling voters things I no longer believed to be true. I often felt I had become a respectable mouthpiece for screwball ideas.

The eternal problem of left-of-centre parties always has been, and always will be, that at some point they will run out of other people's money with which to buy the votes to keep them in office.

As they do now, I then advocated what I called "Keynesianism" (after British economist John Maynard Keynes), calling for increased government expenditure (and, inevitably, concomitant borrowing) to stimulate the economy through consumer spending. But Keynes basically said that governments should spend and borrow in bad times and balance that by repayment of debt in good times. I then, as the left does now, never seemed to find that *any* times were good enough to justify repaying debt, so called for increased spending during all economic circumstances.

I am glad, however, that I did not have the effrontery to call such spending and borrowing "investment" in order to conceal its true nature, as leftists do today.

14: Disillusionment

During the last two years of my time in the Legislature, there were three interesting events connected with work, as opposed to politics.

One was the previously-mentioned need to examine and revise the Rules and Procedures of the House of Assembly which had been in effect for years. I convinced Premier Buchanan that a large committee with a government majority would quickly become partisan and would never produce the required result. Therefore, he agreed to a three person task force, with one person from each party. He appointed my good friend Arthur Donahoe, and the Liberals chose Hugh Tinkham, one of the MLAs for Yarmouth. I represented the NDP on the task force.

It was a long and sometimes arduous task, but we worked extremely well together, all agreeing that the work was in no way partisan and that many of the anachronistic, if not nonsensical, rules from the past had to go. We completely overhauled and streamlined the rules and presented them to the whole House. The Speaker, Ron Russell, allowed Arthur and Hugh to sit on either side of my desk in the centre of the opposition benches, and we took turns in presenting the various sections and the changes we proposed.

Our proposals sailed through, and the changes were unanimously adopted. It was work well done, showing what could happen when politicians of different stripes were dedicated to doing the right thing.

In 1976 Rene Levesque's Parti Quebecois came to power in Quebec on the platform of independence, which naturally gave rise to much speculation, if not fear, about the future of Canada. For this reason (some might say, on this pretext, in view of its perambulations) the House created a Select Committee to delve into constitutional matters, some prominent members of which were Arthur; Jerry Regan; my friend John Leefe, who was the new member for Queens; and Fraser Mooney (Yarmouth) and Bill Gillis (Antigonish) who had been ministers in the previous Liberal administration.

Secretary to the committee was Duncan Fraser, another Dickensian character known sometimes as Doctor, sometimes as Colonel, sometimes as Professor. He was an old pal of the premier's. He was stentorian, pompous and sometimes abusive, strutting around with an enormous leather briefcase embossed with gold letters. Duncan provided us with as much amusement as aggravation as our work proceeded.

For reasons which are even more difficult for me to justify now than they were then, it was felt that the Committee could not complete its work unless it visited the European Economic Community (the forerunner of the E.U.) and the "mother of parliaments" at Westminster. As we approached the NATO headquarters at Brussels, Duncan became *Colonel* Fraser, then *Doctor* Fraser when we later got to the EEC offices.

A number of us were struck by the mind-numbing number (certainly hundreds) of bureaucrats all working away at producing mind-numbing regulations. It was like something from a dystopian science fiction fantasy.

Since then, John Leefe and I have often wondered to what extent that bureaucracy must have grown in the intervening years, and how many thousands of bureaucrats are crafting more regulations to govern people's lives today. The mind boggles at this stultifying organization, which spends $220,091,036,318 annually, while its Parliament costs $2,607,826,314 a year.

At Westminster, we met with my old friend Michael Foot; Lord Hailsham, the Lord Chancellor; and Michael Ryle, one the House of Commons clerks who had come to Nova Scotia to help us recraft our Rules. At one function we were regaled with an orotund history lesson from the famous (some say notorious) Enoch Powell, who bade us look upwards to see the "shining light which is the unbroken link with Edward the Confessor."

There are two anecdotes from this junket. The first is of a trick we played on Duncan, the other of a trick we played on straight-laced Bill Gillis, whom, you will recall, Regan had nicknamed "The Death of the Virgin."

Gillis, Regan, Mooney, one other whose name now escapes me, and I went out to dinner where, by pre-arrangement, I mentioned an alleged brothel nearby which came highly recommended. On cue, the others expressed eagerness to visit the establishment, whereupon poor Bill went as white as a sheet, squirmed in his seat and started stuttering incoherently.

The more salacious enthusiasm we voiced for the venture, the more desperately uncomfortable Bill became. I have never seen anyone so relieved as when we decided we could torture him no longer and told him the place did not even exist.

Jerry thought up the prank on Duncan, who had seen a fine nineteenth century sword in an antique shop nearby. Knowing Duncan to be a fanatic on military matters, his plan was that we would allow Duncan to overhear a conversation in which one of would tell the others that we had been told, on good authority, that this sword had been used by Duke of Wellington, most likely at the Battle of Waterloo, and was a tremendous bargain at the asking price. Jerry would then say he planned to go round and buy it the following day.

It worked like a charm. Duncan rushed out, bought the sword, and lugged the ungainly article back to Canada, where he had to deal with some interesting questions from Customs in Halifax.

~

Another trip I took in that time period was to China and Japan, which had been arranged by the national NDP and the Canadian Labour Congress. I joined a party which was headed by Tommy Douglas, and included Shirley Carr, President of the CLC; MPs David Orlikow and Lorne Nystrom; and Saskatchewan Attorney

General Roy Romanow.

We spent some weeks in China, starting in Beijing, visiting the Great Wall, the magical Kueilin in Guangxi province, Shanghai, Guangzhou, and various other towns and villages, ending up Hong Kong. Throughout, we were treated (if that is the right word) to endless meals (sometimes ten courses) and tedious "tea talks" with Communist Party officials. These were predictable in that they regurgitated the same stuff about friendship between the two nations each time, always mentioning Canada's Dr. Norman Bethune, who was a hero with the Communists, having assisted Mao Ze Dong in the 1930s.

One amusing feature of these interminable events, in which Romanow delighted, was that Tommy could not pronounce Chinese names and, to the obvious embarrassment of the Party officials, insisted on calling Communist Party Chairman, Hua Guofeng "Hog Wog Fang."

At these dinners we were introduced to such delicacies as thousand year old eggs, sea slugs, and Maotai, a ferocious spirit which is distilled from fermented Sorghum, tastes disgusting and administers an instant headache.

Everywhere, we saw the chaos and devastation caused by the brutal excesses of the Cultural Revolution (not entirely dissimilar from the antics of today's fascist left in places like Portland) in which schools and universities were closed, monuments were torn down, children spied and reported on their parents, and people were ripped from their families and shipped thousands of miles to slave camps or farms in Qinghai and even Xinjiang.

All problems in China, we were told, were the fault of the Gang of Four, who headed the Cultural Revolution and comprised Mao's wife, Jiang Qing, Wang Hongwen, Shang Chunqiao, and Yao Wenyuan.

At that time, the Gang of Four were in prison, but had not received a trial. Even though I was under no illusion that if they got a trial it would be anything like a fairly balanced western one, this bothered me and it annoyed Roy Romanow, a lawyer and an attorney general. So, much to Tommy's displeasure (sometimes he embarrassed us by sucking up to the Chinese rather slavishly), whenever questions were called for, Roy and I asked when the Gang of Four would be put on trial. This rattled the officials as much as it did Tommy, and we were put off with pronouncements that "all was in hand" and would be resolved "in the fullness of time." We also received the standard Chinese response to any request they did not want to grant: "Is not convenient".

After we and they repeated this performance many times, finally in Guangzhou, a tall imposing man in a dark business suit (until now all officials we had met, including the Deputy Premier, had worn Mao jackets) burst into our hotel lobby accompanied by half a dozen soldiers bristling with guns. "Romanow! Akerman!" he barked.

Tommy approached him, gushing about Roy and I being the "up and coming" figures in the party, but the man brushed him aside and repeated: "Romanow! Akerman!"

When we raised our hands, he came over to our table and, dismissing both Tommy and his guards, sat down. In perfect English, and with an urbane manner, he told us that we had caused the regime a great of trouble, and for this reason they had decided to hold a trial.

We thanked him. He thanked us and then left.

Some months later the Gang of Four got their trial and were convicted of "anti-party activities". Jiang Qing, the only member of the Gang who bothered to argue on her behalf, was extremely defiant, protesting and shouting. Her argument was that she had obeyed the orders of Mao Zedong at all times. Zhang Chunqiao refused to admit any wrongdoing. Yao Wenyuan and Wang Hongwen expressed repentance and confessed their alleged crimes.

Jiang and Zhang were sentenced to death, Wang got life, and Yao got 20 years.

To us, the current regime was quite restrictive and authoritarian enough, and we were watched over the whole time—'spied' on would be more accurate—and if any of us did anything which was "not convenient" we were sharply rebuked.

Once, Roy and I slipped away from a large dinner at Hongze and sneaked through the dark streets to the huge lake, where we paid a fisherman to take us out for a sail. After a few minutes, we noticed lights coming towards us out of the blackness and we could hear a faint hum. Soon about a dozen boats surrounded us, full of people waving lanterns and singing, "Welcome, Canadian friends".

The next day, when we congratulated the two guides we suspected of being secret police, they grinned broadly, assuming that Roy and I were their equivalents watching over our delegation. From then on, the four of us acted like (but were not really) great buddies.

Once when we had the rare opportunity to have eggs for breakfast (it was usually vegetables), we each gave the time we required the eggs to be boiled. One said three and a half minutes, one said four, others said five. The first egg arrived in three and a half minutes. The next in four minutes, the remainder in five. All were still uncooked.

In our hotel in Kweilin, surely one of the most spectacular places on earth, we found that the showers were spotless and had all the necessary accoutrements, but that nothing was connected to a water supply. Evidently, someone had been sent to the west to get photographs of hospitality facilities, but did not get the information as to how they worked.

Some days before we got to Guangzhou, formerly known as Canton, I came down with a serious streptococcal infection, so our guides arranged for me to see a doctor. He gave me acupuncture, which had no effect, and instructed me to take 30 small, brown, spherical pills every hour (they reminded me of aniseed balls). They were also ineffective.

When we crossed into Hong Kong, I was desperately ill so immediately saw a western physician, who pumped such huge quantities of penicillin into my rear end that I could hardly walk. But within a day I was back on my feet and full of beans, ready to explore a remarkably exciting place.

Hong Kong is basically built on the sides of very tall, very steep mountains, and one evening we went to a party right at the very top of one. There I met a man whose name was something like Augustine Chung. He drove a large, beautiful maroon Rolls Royce and was said to be a billionaire.

When I went out to look across the bay at Kowloon as the sun went down, Mr. Chung followed me out and we talked for quite some time. At one point he told me that if I needed anything, whilst I was there I had only to call upon him. He passed me his card and repeated *anything* with great emphasis.

I thanked him and said I did not think I would need anything out of the ordinary, whereupon he almost gave me a heart attack by saying that if I wanted someone killed, he could take care of that for me, too. Again, I thanked him for his consideration, but politely declined his offer. He gave me a short but spectacular drive in the Rolls, and that was that.

As we went back to the Mandarin Hotel, where we were staying, I wondered if the person who coined the phrase "The Mysterious East" had ever met Mr. Chung.

On our way back from China, we stopped in Tokyo for a few days. Roy, who in addition to being Attorney General, was Minister responsible for the Saskatchewan Potash Corporation, part owner of Canpotex, the company which marketed and exported potash to the world. Canpotex's representative in Japan was a most agreeable man, Mr. Maruhashi, who hived Roy, Nystrom and me away from the delegation to show us a "good time".

It was Sunday and Maruhasi told us all places of entertainment were closed (I have no idea why), so he arranged to have a club/restaurant on the Ghinza open up just for us. When we had eaten our steaks, various seductive young women kept slinking up to the table all, apparently, having English names like Polly, Jenny and Suzy. After a while to my mystification, Roy and Lorne disappeared.

Being a very earnest and conscientious young politician, I continued to ask Maruhashi questions about potash: the quantities which China imported from Saskatchewan, the uses to which it was put, the prices paid, etc. After some time and new young lovelies (called Millie, Rosie and Annie) had come and gone, Maruhashi conspiratorially leaned over and said, "Akerman San, do you want a boy?"

Somewhat embarrassed, and to save face, I continued to grill Maruhashi about potash statistics. Roy and Lorne later returned beaming with happiness. I got heartburn.

~

On our way back from Tokyo, Roy and I had an unpleasant encounter with Prime Minister Trudeau. He was returning from Tibet —he was one of the very few people the Chinese Communists allowed to visit the remote country. He was in a nasty, combative mood, possibly brought on by drink.

Trudeau knew Roy from federal-provincial conferences and greeted him with a sneer, calling him "Roman*off*". He was clearly spoiling for a fight.

Always the gentleman, Roy would not take the bait, so Trudeau turned to me, asking, "Who's your little friend, Romanoff?"

Following an introduction, the prime minister leaned forward and said, "And I suppose you have some problem with me just like everyone else?"

I said I was pleased to meet him and this was neither the time nor the place for arguments, but he insisted.

"Go on, go on, tell me what you have against me."

When pressed, I said that, if he insisted, I thought his most egregious folly was to have invoked the War Measures Act in 1970.

"But I had no choice!" he exploded. "I had to do it because they murdered Pierre LaPorte."

"No, prime minister," I said firmly, "that is a lie. Pierre LaPorte was murdered after you invoked the War Measures, and maybe because of it."

"Fuck you!" Trudeau said and stalked back to the First Class cabin.

I returned to Nova Scotia to find that my house in Glace Bay was almost empty and that Joan had decamped with the furniture to Sydney. I could not blame her; perhaps even more than most politicians I was away from home far more often than I was there.

~

To go into much detail, write about the blood under the bridge, and speak at length about people who were of little consequence and events which no longer matter, if they ever really did, would be tedious for the reader, but the years from 1978 to 1980 were unpleasant and disillusioning in the extreme. Those who either wanted me out and/or were out-and-out Marxists took over offices in the party. The NDP, like all western left of centre parties, had been changing for some time from a movement dedicated to the poor and working class into a rag-bag coalition of what Paul MacEwan called "one issue obsessionists", all strident, all intolerant, and all vicious. For a party which claimed a monopoly on compassion and caring, it had far more than its fair share of downright nasty and savage zealots for whom the ends justified any means, no matter how underhanded or dishonest.

Where once miners, steelworkers, carpenters, farmers and the like sat around the tables, now it was social workers, lawyers and university professors. Where once debates were about wages, working conditions, health care and pensions, now they were about abortion, changing names to appease feminists, ecological alarmism, and various "rights" for this or that group, gender, race or ethnicity. Where once left-of-centre parties identified with the underdog of all underdogs, Israel, now they became anti-Semitic, urging an unholy alliance with Islamists. Where once they had been somewhat critical but supportive of western Judaeo-Christian civilization, now they became hostile to it, blaming it for all the world's problems. Where once they had been allied to Christianity, with leaders like Tommy Douglas who were clergymen, now Christianity was sneered at and denigrated as "right wing".

I saw it as another kind of Cultural Revolution, one which is continuing today with the insanity of tearing down statues of people which were erected not as a mark of approval for every word they uttered or every action they took, but because their subjects were integral to and instrumental in society's development.

This was not what I signed up for, and my state of mind in no way eased when, in the winter of 1978-79, I had helped my old friend Michael Foot in his office in London when he was Deputy Prime Minister to Jim Callaghan. In Britain it was called "The Winter of Discontent", and it manifested itself in mass strikes across the country, even to the point where corpses lay unburied and garbage piled up high in streets.

To get to my parents' place 100 miles away from London, normally a drive of two hours, I had to zigzag back and forth across country to get a gallon of gas here and there, wherever garages had any fuel left to offer. It took me almost five hours to get there.

The main protagonists were the Labour government and the unions, the majority of which were on strike mostly for more money. The public sector unions had demanded more than Jim Callaghan thought the government could afford (it was hugely in debt, and was already levying high taxes). The largest and most vociferous of these unions was the Transport and General Workers Union, headed by Moss Evans, who presided over more than two million members and was seen as the spokesman for everyone who was on strike.

It was absolute chaos—like a runaway train carrying nuclear material—with neither the government nor the unions budging, and neither with any clue what to do next or how to get out of the mess.

At Question Time I would sit in the Speaker's Gallery and watch while a wretched, coiffured, shrill, harridan eviscerated the government day after day. I loathed her. Her name was Margaret Thatcher. But as the days passed, she wore me down, because I knew what was going on upstairs, and I knew in my heart that she was right: no government can allow itself to be held to ransom.

I would sit around the office with Michael Foot, Chief Whip Michael Cocks, his deputy Walter Harrison, Michael's Parliamentary

Private Secretary, Caerwyn Roderick, and Chancellor Dennis Healey as they moaned and wrung their hands.

One day Jim dropped by and said a decision had to be made. He asked the room (not me, of course) what the government should do. The response was that he should check with Moss Evans to see if it was all right with him.

At that moment it was clear that the government of the United Kingdom was not in this room, but in a room four blocks away at Transport House in Smith Square.

Mrs. Thatcher had been right all along. Only the elected government should govern, and *must* govern; no outside organization or alliance of pressure groups should ever be allowed to usurp that constitutional authority.

A few days later, the government fell on a no-confidence vote and the country went to the polls. Mrs. T. won 339 seats, picking up 62. Poor Jim lost 50 seats. The Labour Party would not govern again for 18 years.

~

In 1979 there was also a federal election in Canada, in which Andy Hogan romped home in his riding with over 15,000 votes while the party picked up 9 seats. The Tories' Joe Clark got the most seats with 136 so it was a minority government and not likely to last.

It clung on until the following February, when Canada went back to the polls. This time Pierre Trudeau's Liberals won a majority of 14 seats. Although the NDP jumped up to 35 seats, Hogan did not re-join them.

I feared bad news might be in the wind when, at our most recent national convention, I had noticed that Hogan was practically living in the bar. To say he ran a bad campaign would not be accurate because he ran virtually *no* campaign. Worse, without consulting us at headquarters he would undertake to speak to schools and organizations, then fail to show up. He was unreachable most of the time, cloistering himself at St. Anne's rectory in Glace Bay where, I have no doubt, he was drinking heavily.

At the same time, the Liberal candidate, young David Dingwall, was out working like a dervish, knocking on doors and dashing hither and thither. I could smell it in the air, and when I asked PeeWee Gillis, "Is Andy OK in new Waterford?" and he replied, "No, B'y", I knew it was all over.

I called the gang together and warned them what to expect. They laughed at me.

But Hogan himself knew. He called me at the headquarters in the late afternoon of election day and asked, "Jerry, how many am I going lose by?"

Barely able to be civil to him I replied, "About 300".

He hung up.

I was three votes out: Dingwall won by 297 votes. Hogan had squandered a majority of 5,012 in just one year.

I never saw him again, never forgave him and never missed him

~

Throughout my years in politics I was fortunate to have a great friend in Sidney Green of Winnipeg, whom I saw at Federal Council and Executive meetings across the country. Sid was an MLA and for some time a member of Ed Schreyer's cabinet. A man of great principle, who had a wonderful sense of humour, was excellent company, and was an endless source of Jewish jokes.

You can read about Sid's adventures and misadventures in detail in his book, *Rise and Fall of a Political Animal*, which I highly recommend. We had many laughs together, often at the expense of other members of the Executive, whom we would imitate as well as imitating each other.

One escapade in which Sidney involved me was one which, in retrospect, I think was misguided. Sidney's recollections and mine differ somewhat as to the details, but here is the broad outline of the affair, as I remember it.

We called it Operation Big K. The party was looking for a new leader as David Lewis was stepping down, and Sid conceived the idea that former Liberal cabinet minister Eric Kierans would be a good choice. At the time Sid convinced me, so we went to work, never asking anyone if they thought he could win, but only if they would personally support him.

When we had a goodly number committed, we approached Kierans and said, "We are going to say something *to which we do not want you to respond."* We told him what we wanted to do, and said we would go out and find further supporters and come back to him with a request that he meet with them.

Following our request, Kierans said not a word, which told us he was definitely interested. Later we returned and asked if he would attend a dinner at the Chateau Laurier hotel in Ottawa. He agreed.

At that time, Ed Broadbent had just announced that he would not seek the leadership because he wanted to spend more time listening to Bach. Kierans said, "That's an interesting gimmick."

Around that time, when I was in a Gents' toilet, Broadbent, who had got wind of Operation Big K, stormed in and in a furious rage started shouting at me, calling me a "goddamn Liberal". Then I knew he had been lying about listening to Bach; he desperately wanted to be Leader.

There were people at the dinner who later denied they were there and some who wished they had not been there, but my recollection is there were about thirty, all holding relatively senior positions in the party. I recall the heads of two of Canada's largest unions, Lloyd Shaw (Alexa McDonough's father), Charles Taylor, Quebec leader Henri Francois Gautrin (later a Liberal MNA and cabinet minister), Manitoba Premier Ed Schreyer, and others.

We said we would go around the table and have each person say why they thought Kierans fitted the bill, but that we still did not want Kierans to respond. At the end of the meal it looked encouraging because neither then, nor at any other time, did Kierans tell us to stop.

In the event, Broadbent changed his mind, as we knew he would, and many of those who had pledged support for Kierans reneged and ran. We did not go back to Kierans, the whole scheme evaporated, and Broadbent became the leader. (Wikipedia's entry that Kierans "considered running for the leadership of the New Democratic Party in 1975 but declined in favour of Ed Broadbent" is as funny as it is false.)

At the time I was disappointed, but I do not think Kierans would have gained the party a significant number of new voters and, more to the point, nor do I think he would have got along at all well with Sidney and myself.

Some years later, when Kierans was appointed by the Nova Scotia government to head up a commission on the Constitution, I appeared before them to make a reasoned presentation. At the beginning of the session, Kierans asked those with sizable briefs to wait until after verbal presentations had been made, so I did as he asked. But when that time came and I rose to make my presentation, Kierans cut me off, saying they had run out of time, which was quite false.

I protested and called him "Eric", but he pretended not to know me. Also, in a book he wrote, he dismissed Sidney and me as lightweights whose proposal he had never seriously considered, which was also a lie.

Sidney and I are still in touch, and he helped me with this section. At time of writing he is 92 and still living in Winnipeg.

~

Apart from Paul MacEwan's 1976 history, *Miners and Steelworkers: Labour in Cape Breton*, there was little available to tell the story of the Island's working class. Charles Lipton mentioned Cape Breton in his 1966 *The Trade Union Movement in Canada*, but the book's scope did not allow for much local detail and it dealt with history only up to 1959.

In, I think, the early 1950s, District 26 of the United Mineworkers of America commissioned a C. B. Wade to write the union's colourful history, and it was to the remnants of this unpublished work that MacEwan had access and which he subsequently passed on to me. It was a mess because, while the research was a treasure trove of information, the hundreds of poorly-typed pages were un-numbered and hopelessly mixed up.

But with perseverance and patience, what a tale it revealed of violence, deprivation, struggle and a way of life which was precarious at best and short and brutish at worst.

After I had ploughed through Wade's work, I realized that in its existing form it could never see the light of day and, in any event, Paul had already used the essential details in his book. What was needed, I determined, was something which gave life to the statistics and saw these extraordinary events through the eyes of the people who lived and suffered through them.

Thus, in the late summer of 1978, I decided to write a novel based upon historical events, but not unduly wedded to boring facts and figures. The trouble was that we guessed a provincial election was coming which would completely take up my time and energies.

So I asked my friend Charlie Joe Gallant if he could lend me his farmhouse at Belle Côte in Inverness County, so I could do the project before being carried off to the hustings. Fortunately, his extensive family would not be using the place all summer and he said he could fit me in for two weeks.

The place was old, creaky and had no electricity or running water, but was isolated and as quiet as the grave. Here I took my tiny, tinny Olivetti portable typewriter and, by natural light by day and by oil lamp at night, I set to putting flesh on the bones of the incredible trials and tribulations of the miners of Glace Bay and surrounding areas.

Working day and night, I completed my task by the time I had to surrender the farmhouse to Charlie Joe's family. And just in time it was, too, because Premier Regan had called a provincial election for September 19. That, and other events I have mentioned, caused me to put aside, and almost forget, the manuscript until almost two years later.

The book's narrator was one Donnie Ross, a coal miner from a mythical area called "The Dump" (based on The Hub in Glace Bay), and it is from his perspective we learn about the strikes and lockouts which marked the period. The book presented a dichotomy between the romance and the reality of those times. The noble ideas espoused by the working classes of Cape Breton inevitably clashed with the status quo, and it was a battle they could only partially win and then after many decades. In Cape Breton in 1925 I think no sane, feeling person could not have been a Communist, Today I think no sane person could be.

After I got out of politics in the fall of 1980, I retrieved the manuscript from the box in which it had sat for so long and sent it to my friend, author Silver Donald Cameron, under the pretense that it had been written by an old, retired coal miner who had lived through the events described.

Enthused beyond measure he arrived at my house in Glace Bay with Jack McClelland (of the publishing house McLelland and Stewart) in tow, demanding to meet the non-existent "Donald Ross". Over cups of tea I explained that there was no Donnie Ross and that I was the author.

Almost instantly they lost interest. They stuck to their word that it would be published, but did virtually no promotion. The golden words of the working-class hero they had worshipped were now but the dross of a politician. I appeared on a few radio talk shows, but that was about it.

I seem to recall that the book, with the title *Black Around the Eyes*, and which was overpriced for the times at $15, sold a little more than 2,000 copies.

~

In the fall of 1980 a series of events crystallized my thinking. In insulting terms, various party officials told me I was "under-performing embarrassingly", that my "body language was wrong", and that I had been sexist when I pointed out that legislature committees were comprised of uneven numbers, so it was impossible to demand they be half men and half women as they insisted.

Added to which was that, encouraged by the Marxists, the

party's provincial secretary, who had been previously been my personal secretary, decided that it was her prerogative to use her office as an Official Opposition to the Leader and Caucus. This became known as the battle between Church and State.

People on the party payroll abandoned the neutrality required by their positions to openly campaign for candidates running for various positions at conventions. And the president, Bob Levy (later an MLA), whom I had cultivated, brought into the party, and took for a friend and ally, started snarling and growling at me. Enough, I thought, enough.

So, I decided I had had a bellyful of wasting my time with nonsensical garbage, and with malcontents, not to mention fronting for an outfit which was essentially hypocritical and offering incessant spending, taxing and borrowing. I called Rollie Thornhill, who was then Minister of Development. We met and told him I wanted out.

He spoke with the premier who then asked me to become Executive Director of Intergovernmental Affairs, which included matters dealing with the Constitution. I accepted, and on October 14, 1980, ten years and one day after I was elected, I submitted my resignation from the House to the Speaker.

After I had announced that I would be stepping down, all hell broke loose because, when asked by reporters why I was going, Paul MacEwan, said he thought it was because "Trotskyites" were active in the party, something the media transformed into "Communists".

In those days the NDP was, understandably, terrified of being associated with Communism due to the appalling record of misery and death Communist regimes had bequeathed around the world, and not least because the party has always harboured a minority of members who were considerably to the left of the party mainstream. That was true in Nova Scotia, although they were few, and the people to whom Paul referred were Marxists, but not of Trotskyite variety.

The distinction between the two harks back to 1928 when Stalin banished Leon Trotsky from the USSR for advocating "permanent revolution" (meaning in more than one country simultaneously), as opposed to the Russian Communist Party's policy of "consolidation" in Russia. In Canada, the Trotskyites were very troublesome because they were known for secret infiltration and, once embedded in the NDP, causing havoc.

In an act of stupendous folly and supreme irony, the party decided to undertake an action of which Stalin himself would have been proud: they staged a "show trial", put MacEwan in the dock, and dragged in David Lewis to act as prosecutor, judge and jury. It was a farce and a travesty, and delivered the predetermined verdict: Paul was guilty and was expelled.

I completely understand why they were mad at Paul, but to react in this manner was as outrageous as it was dishonest and corrupt. In Cape Breton, it took them years to recover from this insanity, all four seats being lost to the party until 1998, when my friend and former constituency president Reeves Matheson won back my seat of Cape Breton East.

MacEwan continued to get elected in Cape Breton Nova under various tickets until 2003, when he retired from politics.

~

I withdrew and resigned in the way I did because I was afraid that if my good people in Glace Bay had the chance to get me to change my mind, I might give in and be right back in the nightmare imbroglio. In retrospect, I should have done it very differently.

After resigning from the NDP, I should have announced that, at my constituency office, I would be holding a poll at which anyone on the 1978 voters' list could cast a ballot. They would have three options:

1. Should I sit as an Independent?
2. Should I apply for membership in the Government caucus?
3. Should I apply for membership in the Liberal caucus?

There is no way of knowing how they would have voted, but I suspect most would have gone for Option 2.

Regardless, I am confident that, had I taken that course of action, there is a very good chance I would still be sitting in the Legislature. Perhaps more interesting and gratifying than self-flattery, is that a number of times over the years both Gerald Regan and Gerald Doucet told me that had I done it that way, I would eventually have become premier. A former finance minister, Neil LeBlanc, also expressed similar sentiments to me.

15: Life with John

When I accepted Premier John Buchanan's offer to head up the Intergovernmental Affairs department, I was so sick of the strife in the NDP, and was so desperate to get out, that I grabbed it without getting proper agreement about the job, the department and the salary. John asked me how much I wanted, to which I replied I would take the average amount of the deputy ministers' remuneration, and that when they received increases, I would get them also.

John agreed, but it was verbal, I foolishly not asking to get it in writing, with the result that, over the next ten years, the deputies' salaries increased dramatically, while mine did not. A number of promises to correct this from the premier and various Ministers of Management Board, like Ron Russell, were never kept.

John seemed to think that there was a treasure chest of money available to Nova Scotia from the Government of Canada which we had not identified, and that we were therefore losing out on many millions. This, he said, was to be my main task; but I was also to be involved in federal-provincial conferences, Council of Maritime Premiers' meetings, gatherings of the Atlantic Premiers and New England Governors, and, should events require it, responding to constitutional matters.

In the event, I quickly discovered that any line department not being run by total idiots would find and extract every penny available to them from Ottawa, so I never had to fulfill that aspect of the job.

The rest of the job description accurately described what I did until the point when I became convinced that the department was a waste of taxpayers' money and told John he should disband it. He was aghast, and the deputy ministers were incredulous: Neither could believe that anyone would ask for his own department, and his job, to be abolished. Apparently, it had never happened before in Nova Scotia government history.

Shrugging his shoulders, John signed the department's death warrant and moved me to the Policy Board as second in command to Deputy Minister Carmen Moir, a devoutly religious bureaucrat's bureaucrat, with whom I got along extremely well, although I was never sure how much I could trust him.

Nominally, my minister at Intergovernmental Affairs was Edmund Morris. I say "nominally" because, in dealing with other governments, the only person who can (and should) handle matters is the premier himself. Therefore, any decisions Edmund made were always subject to countermand by the Boss.

However, this did not stop Edmund from exercising considerable discretion in ordering that strange things be carried out, and in doing strange things himself. This led to occasional conflicts between us.

One of them arose over his installing the son of a well-known Tory in the department, where I discovered he was conducting an insurance and real estate business while receiving a government salary. When I saw an ad for his business in the *Chronicle Herald* giving a government phone number for prospective clients to contact, I did not care whose toes I trod on, and ordered him to pull the phone number forthwith. Edmund was not amused, but he knew it was scandalous and that I was correct.

Another occasion on which we had a showdown was when, without informing me, his secretary organized an office Christmas party and ordered quantities of liquor. As soon as I heard about it, I stopped the order and, when Edmund demanded to know why I had done so, I gave it to him with both barrels: The idea that the taxpayers should pay for alcohol to be consumed by civil servants in offices to which the public had free access was outlandishly improper on every level. He correctly asserted that he was the minister and would have his way, whereupon I said I would gladly refer the matter to the premier for adjudication. He backed off instantly.

But most of the time our interactions were just amusing or bizarre. Once, when I had a meeting with my fellow Intergovernmental deputies in Montreal, Edmund, knowing full well this was an officials-only meeting, showed up out of the blue bearing masses of lobsters, bought at public expense for the assembled company. The officials were bewildered, but ate the lobsters!

Although he had entirely unnecessarily spent public money on lobsters, airfare and a hotel room, he upbraided me at breakfast the next morning for having bacon and eggs instead of porridge, saying I should have more consideration for the taxpayers.

Another of these bizarre events occurred when the Spanish Ambassador was visiting Nova Scotia and I arranged for a brief, *pro forma* meeting with Edmund. When the ambassador came, I took him over to the Legislature, went up to the gallery, scrawled a note and had the messenger take it down to Edmund. It said:

Edmund: The Ambassador is here.

Edmund opened the note, wrote on it for what seemed like many minutes, handed it to the page to bring up to me, and turned back to read some reports on his desk. When the note was returned to me, I saw that he had crossed out my message and in its place, taking both sides of the paper, had written:

Minister: His Excellency the Ambassador for Spain (then the man's full name) is without and waiting upon attendance.

But he did not move.

I sent down another note:

Here. Now. Lobby. Go.

He looked at the note, frowned deeply and, clearly annoyed, huffed his way to the door.

When the United Appeal was doing its rounds in the halls of

government. I mildly expressed my reservation about donating to an umbrella organization which, among worthy causes, included some recipients of which some civil servants might not approve. His mouth opened and shut with amazement. Then he said, "Jeremy, I am surprised at your unordinary parsimony. We must all be effortful in our eleemosynary activities."

~

This was the time when Prime Minister Pierre Trudeau turned his attention toward a lifelong goal: to bring home the Canadian constitution. The British North America Act, which had brought Canada into being in 1867, was a statute of the British Parliament. Trudeau was determined to bring home a revised constitution so Canadians no longer needed Britain's approval in order to change it. His vision of the Constitution included a charter of rights and freedoms, which he said would protect citizens against arbitrary actions by their governments.

But Trudeau's dream was not shared by all, me among them. Most provincial premiers opposed Trudeau's sweeping charter of rights proposal. They correctly feared it would diminish their influence, transferring power from elected politicians to non-elected judges. Ontario and New Brunswick agreed to go along with Ottawa, but the others, "The Gang of Eight" did not.

When Trudeau threatened to take his case directly to London, each of the dissenting provinces sent their heads of Intergovernmental Affairs to Britain to lobby for support to defeat Trudeau should the matter come to the floors of the Houses of Commons and Lords at Westminster.

So I headed off to London with my counterparts, including an old friend, Howard Leeson, from Saskatchewan, and new ones, Peter Meekison from Alberta and Robert Normand from Quebec. After a while I was given a Tory worker, Steve Probyn, to assist me as we met with and tried to convince MPs and peers of all parties to back our side.

One problem which immediately arose was that the provinces

all had Agents General in London, whose main job it was to drum up trade, but who incorrectly imagined that we were answerable to them, and should defer to them as to whom we met and what we should say. This was a recipe for disaster, not only because they were rank amateurs in the field (except one: Gilles Loiselle of Quebec), but because they had all been political buddies of the premiers who appointed them as rewards for party services rendered.

To undermine any initiative we deputies had devised (and the Agents General repeatedly tried to undermine our efforts), all it took was for one of the AGs to call his premier and feed him a load of nonsense and gossip, knowing it would soon pass on to the other premiers.

Unfortunately, Nova Scotia had the worst Agent General in Donald Smith, who had been a Tory MLA from Halifax for ten years. Smith was myopic, narrow-minded, cantankerous, uncooperative, even abusive, and he made it abundantly clear that he was prepared to sabotage the Gang of Eight's efforts unless the deputies handed everything over to his club of buddies. This would have negated the purpose for our visit, since some of the AGs did not themselves believe their provinces were doing the right thing, and thought that it was demeaning and brash to actually lobby Members of Parliament.

We deputies were quite certain at that point that if the matter did come to a vote in the Commons, we would win. We had the numbers, but we had no idea how long we would keep them before the old boys' club took over.

After a while, it became clear that there was dissension in the ranks at home, with some provinces weakening, so I left Probyn to do what he could and returned to try to steel the premier's resolve to stick with it and not give in to Trudeau. Eventually, the coalition fell apart and a deal was signed in Ottawa which included the infamous Charter of Rights. It was done without Quebec's participation—or even with their immediate knowledge—and years of rancour followed.

Probyn returned after running up horrendous bills which he

presented to me to pay, many of them having been expenses incurred or encouraged by the egregious Donald Smith. Since I neither agreed with nor had authorized these expenses, I called the Auditor General, Arnold Sarty, and asked his advice. He told me to send them to the premier, which I did. John never mentioned them to me, which suggested that he viewed them with equal disapproval. Later I made discreet inquiries and discovered that John had just handed them all to the Deputy Minister of Finance, saying,"Make these disappear."

Another constitutional adventure worth recording concerned yet another federal-provincial wrangle, the outcome of which the media reported along the lines of: *Quebec Premier outraged not consulted on Agreement.*

To cut a tediously long story short, on the ultimate night of the conference, days of arguing had resulted in Premier René Levesque leaving the meeting apparently exasperated (he was a great actor), and telling the others to be sure to phone him when they had put together the wording of the agreement and communique. Simultaneously with that occurrence, my Quebec counterpart and friend, Robert Normand, invited me into Levesque's suite for a drink.

No sooner had I the glass in my hand than the doors burst open and the premier and his entourage swept into the room. Within minutes, a man stood up and started barking orders. I asked Robert what was going on.

He said, "I am sorry, Jeremy, but you are here for the night. All the doors are being locked and all the phones are being disconnected. I can't go into details but these are orders from the Boss."

When, a little sore and a little hung over, I stumbled through the hotel lobby in the morning, I saw the headlines. The others had not contacted him about the wording of the agreement and communique, Levesque complained bitterly that this was typical of the contempt with which they always treated Quebec.

And, of course, it was true: They had not contacted him because, by deliberate design, he had been incommunicado all night.

~

Whenever the premier travelled to any meeting which involved other governments, he always wanted me to go with him, although, to be frank, what use I was on those occasions is highly questionable. When he was away from home in strange places, I think John felt more comfortable if familiar faces surrounded him. Usually, that would be the late Dennis Ashworth, his senior assistant, Joe Clarke, secretary to cabinet, myself and an official of one of the departments.

Usually, we travelled to these events on what the Opposition insisted on calling the "luxury government jet", which was neither luxurious nor a jet. Sometimes, we would pick up PEI premier Jim Lee (and take him home on the way back) and one of his staff, and when the seats were filled either Joe or I sat on the toilet. The plane was cramped, and very, very slow.

Sometimes, we travelled by car, in which case John would have us stop at every filling station diner, go in, glad-hand all present, and then go on our way. Naturally, this performance stopped at the New Brunswick border.

It often seemed that when we were away, my chief job was to have breakfast with him, so he could gossip about his cabinet and go through the morning paper with me, analyzing various stories. He would come to the table asking, "Which of my ministers has embarrassed me today?"

Once, I read him a news story in which George Henley had made a controversial comment and, with George's typical, down-to-earth frankness, added something to the effect that he might not be in cabinet for long. "That can be arranged!" John said decisively.

When we were away, John always seemed to be in desperate need of shirts and aftershave lotion. I never used the latter, but no matter how many times I told him, he would still call my room looking for some. When he wanted a shirt (always plain—no stripes or bright colours) various members of staff would be dispatched into the town to buy several. The first time he asked me, I politely pointed out that I had noticed that when others did this for him they were never reimbursed. He laughed, but took the point and never asked me again.

How he could suffer to wear stiff, brand new shirts straight out of the plastic, I never understood, but it might have explained why he was constantly holding his tie knot and stretching his neck.

Whenever the premier had to give a speech or make a presentation, Joe and I would do our best to write something short, snappy, and with a point to make. Invariably, John would change everything, so that it said nothing, but took twice as long to deliver.

He asked me why, at Federal-Provincial conferences, other premiers got all kinds of media attention but he never did. I told him it was because he never said anything. He looked startled.

But it was true. Usually, all he said was that Nova Scotia was a wonderful place, and that everyone should visit us. Then he would go around the table handing his counterparts Nova Scotia tartan ties, mugs, or some nautical memento.

At one of these national conferences, the staff brought around the transcripts of the previous day's proceedings. I extracted John's speech and passed it to him.

"Here's your speech," I said.

John grabbed it, started to read, frowned, then took out his pen and began to cross out words and sentences and scrawl in the margins.

"What are you doing, John?"

"This is wrong," he replied, "I can't say this."

"But you did say it."

"What do you mean?"

"This is not a draft for a speech for you to give today. It is the speech you gave yesterday."

"What? It's all wrong." He pointed to various sections with his pen.

"But, this is the word-for-word record of what you said yesterday."

"Can I change it?"

"No, you can't change the verbatim transcript"

John shook his head and used the expression he always did when he felt further effort to be fruitless: "Waddya gonna do?"

~

At these out of town meetings and conferences, New Brunswick premier Richard Hatfield would be in attendance and, after the proceedings ended for the day, he and I would get together, drink scotch and talk until the early hours of the morning. He was a curious man, one of the strangest I have ever known; a mass of contradictions, very bright but mentally disorganized.

For someone who had been over 20 years in politics and had been premier for over a dozen, he did not seem particularly interested in governing. He and told me he spent as little time in New Brunswick as possible, preferring such places as Algiers and Marrakesh.

Named after Prime Minister R.B. Bennett, Richard told many tales about his namesake. including his alleged farewell speech from the top of the gangplank of the ship which took him to England, where he lived out the rest of his life. According to Dick, the former PM addressed the porter and two other people standing on the wharf with the following incongruous malapropisms: "The topmost rung of life's ambition no longer shines with the brightest light. The plaudits of the crowd are no longer music to my ears."

Hatfield also spoke much about his father, who had been an MP for 12 years, and how "they" had plotted against him in "dastardly fashion". I never understood what this was all about because, while he could drink phenomenal amounts of scotch, he would be well into his cups whenever he talked about his father.

In private, many whispered about Dick's sexual orientation, which only began to be openly discussed in media and biographical writing after his death. He once was quoted as saying: "the nuclear family—one wife, two kids and one dog—looks nice on Christmas cards, but they pay an awful price."

I neither knew nor cared because I liked Richard enormously

and greatly enjoyed his company. As Churchill is supposed to have said about W, Somerset Maugham, "I know what they say about Willy, but he's never tried to bugger me."

Meeting as we sometimes did, in out of the way places like Bouctouche or Pokemouche, it seemed hilarious to me that Richard often fantasized about our going out into the blackness and finding an all-night bar. He died at age 60 from a brain tumour, and wherever he is, I hope he found that bar.

~

John Buchanan was what is called a "people person". He loved shaking hands, slapping backs, working the crowd, going to rubber chicken dinners, and making voters feel good. At Gerry Ritcey's funeral in Truro, eleven years after John left the premiership, we all waited while the proceedings were held up because John was glad-handing and hugging mourners in the lobby.

He could no more resist interacting with everybody in sight than fly to the moon. And he often backed away from decisions or actions because they might hurt individuals, because strife and dissension might result, or because he disliked confrontation.

This was why he frequently allowed civil servants to get away with insolent behaviour, a phenomenon most often seen in the appalling disrespect his chauffeur, Jack Wheatley, showed to him and to his wife, Mavis, whom he refused to drive to the airport on one occasion because he said she was not a public servant. In the event, John and I went in the car with Wheatley, while Mavis had to go by taxi.

I often asked John, "Why don't you fire him?"

To which John shrugged and said, "Waddya gonna do?"

When John had asked me to prepare a cross-indexed, digest document about the offshore oil and gas industry to which he could make rapid reference in meetings, my assistant, Scott Brison (later an MP and federal cabinet minister) and I found every answer but one. We asked the Deputy Minister of Energy for the figure, but he absolutely refused to supply it even though they knew it was for the premier.

When I told John, he shook his head and said, "Waddya gonna do? Jeremy, you know what people are like."

On another occasion, John had determined to establish an arms-length, grant-making Arts Council, something for which the community had been asking for years, and asked if I would head it. Just when everything seemed ready to go, John called me and said he could not go ahead with it because the Department of Culture and Recreation was "up in arms" and refused to implement it. Years later, in the grocery store, I met Allison Bishop, one of the department's senior civil servants, and asked him why they blocked it. He was quite candid: "Because the idea did not originate with us."

That attitude was by no means atypical of the Nova Scotia civil service at that time. In many respects, I thought it mirrored quite closely the biting British comedy series *Yes, Minister*.

At one point, John and I established a record for his making, and my accepting, seven appointments in one day, all of which he had rescinded by midnight. They ranged across the government spectrum from museums to industrial development, and it was clear that in every case, either the ministers or departments concerned blocked the order.

One appointment he wanted to make, but which I could not accept, was for a new Deputy Agent General in London. When I was on vacation in Britain, I spent a few days at the Province's offices in Pall Mall, and mentioned to the staff the possibility that the premier might bring in someone as deputy to the odious Donald Smith. To a person, they objected strenuously (as each of them thought they should get the job), so I realized it could not work.

When I told John, he said, "Huh, that's the second job you've talked yourself out of."

It was not only towards the premier that civil servants could be insolent; some treated ministers with equal disrespect. When I was first appointed to Intergovernmental Affairs, I made the rounds of the deputy ministers in the various departments. At the curiously misnamed Department of Transportation, I met long-time deputy Bill Kerr, who showed me around. As we passed the open door of the minister, Tom McInnis (later a Senator), Kerr said loudly, "This is where we keep the idiot. Don't waste your time with him".

I was mortified and, looking through the doorway, could see Tom's pained expression. He was a very decent man and did not deserve treatment like that from a thug like Kerr.

I told John what had happened and said he should kick Kerr out, but he shrugged, saying, "Waddya gonna do? You know what people are like."

~

I am guessing that history will record that, while John was one of the most popular premiers of all time, and that he was always sympathetic to appeals from individuals and groups, his greatest failure was not keeping the province's finances in good order. He ran up an enormous debt, for some of which our grandchildren and their children will be burdened in terms of higher taxation and/or fewer/poorer public services.

There were a number of reasons for what he did, one of which he explained to me when I told him that I thought the fiscal situation was getting out of control. He replied that he had been advised by local developer and millionaire, Joe Zatzman, that because inflation would continue at a high rate for many years, the province could borrow as much as it wanted now because when it came time to repay it would cost us almost nothing.

I thought this was so utterly ludicrous, I walked away in a daze of disbelief.

But bad, or misinterpreted, advice was not the main reason for profligate borrowing, only its justification. The real reason was that John was so kindly, he wanted to give people everything they wanted. He could not say "no" to a request if it were dressed up as a dire need and accompanied with flattering comments.

When the Policy Board (of which I was Secretary) was meeting one day, the door opened and a beckoning hand appeared. I went out to find John standing there. He said he was temporarily appointing me Secretary to the Executive Council (cabinet) and I was to go back in, announce that appointment, and say that Policy Board was resolving itself into a session of cabinet, whereupon he would enter.

When I pointed out that there were insufficient ministers in the room to form a quorum of cabinet, he cutely said he had the others' proxies in his back pocket. So in I went and did what I was instructed.

The chairman, the estimable Terry Donahoe, grinned from ear to ear, guessing what was going to happen, and called out, "God love you Premier, why don't you join us?"

John entered as though it were just a casual visit and sat down. He said that he had been in Yarmouth the evening before and that they had given him a "wonderful reception". He said they badly needed a new gym for the school, and that he had promised to deliver it.

When Terry, who was also Minister of Education, said that the project was not on the department's priority list, John said, "Yeah, Terry, but they gave me a fantastic reception. You should have seen it."

Terry smiled and shrugged, so John leaned across the table to Finance Minister, Greg Kerr, saying, "Greg, go across the road and float a bond issue in Germany for $5 million."

Greg jumped up, grabbed his briefcase and left.

John turned to me. "Jeremy, your appointment is rescinded."

~

For a number of the years I worked for John, his senior assistant/advisor was an enigmatic lawyer, Fred Dickson, whom John called 'Dicks', who (highly questionably) continued to execute his instructions within government after he had left the public service and was back in private practice. Impossible to dislike, Fred had an inscrutable smile, spoke in halting undertones, and when annoyed broke pencils and threw them in the air.

He enjoyed the premier's total confidence, having his fingers—and hands—in many of the government's activities, but he did not always communicate as lucidly as might be desired, as will be seen by this story.

At a much heralded press conference, John announced what was billed as "the greatest reorganization of government in the history of the province." Like all government reorganizations, this was largely smoke and mirrors, leaving functions and duties in place but transferring them to the jurisdiction of different departments.

But there were several agencies which were not included in the list and this, naturally, this sparked questions from the media. John was clearly nonplussed and, unable to explain the omissions, hastily said he would look into it and left.

Later that day, he called me and asked me if I would go with him to a reopening of Chinatown, a restaurant on the Bedford Highway. During the dinner he pulled me aside and took me behind some heavy plush drapes.

"What did you think of the re-organization?" he asked.

"Very embarrassing," I replied, "a total disaster."

"Yeah."

"What happened?"

"Dicks did it," he almost wailed. "It was Dicks' fault."

"You mean someone who doesn't even work for the government, restructured the government? Jesus, John, that's a real mess."

"I know," John said. "Waddya gonna do?"

~

Despite his propensity for hugging and black slapping, some people saw John Buchanan as a man who never showed his feelings. But I did not share that opinion because, in private at least, he often made no secret of them. And once I saw him cry.

It was in 1986 when Billy Joe MacLean, MLA for Inverness South, had been found guilty of forgery and fiddling his expenses, and all manner of sanctimonious, high minded individuals were demanding that he be ejected from the Legislature.

Consequently, the government had introduced a law which expelled him from the Legislature and prohibited him from seeking re-election for five years. The legislation was worded in a general way so as to be applicable to any Member who was guilty of an offence which warranted a jail term of five years or more, but dress it up though they might, it was clearly the Billy Joe MacLean Act, targeting one man.

I told John that hard cases always make bad law, but beyond that objection, that the idea was repugnant that the House could decide its own membership by dint of a majority vote. I felt the precedent was extremely dangerous and could be abused by some future totalitarian government. I said that the government should withdraw the legislation and let the voters in his district decide his fate at the next election.

John did not disagree but said he had to do it because "the clergy" were giving him a hard time. He loved Billy Joe like a brother, and it was apparent that having to take this action was tearing him apart.

I said, "Don't do it."

He wept as he repeated, "I've got to do it."

The House was unanimous in passing the bill, even Paul MacEwan, who should have taken a principled stand, voting for it. In the event, in January of the next year the Supreme Court struck down the section which prohibited Billy Joe from running again as unconstitutional, and in a by-election a month later the people of Inverness South sent him back to the legislature. John was delighted, but a year after that Billy Joe was defeated in the general election.

~

What I perceived as one of John's weaknesses was his habit of assigning the same task to different people without telling them there were others on the case, which had the effect of confusing him and creating bad blood within the ranks. One example of this had undesired if amusing results when he called me early one morning asking me if I would go out to the house and help his daughter, Natasha, with an essay she had to write for her history teacher.

I duly went out to Spryfield and sat down with her to find that the essay was to be about the British Prime Minister, Benjamin Disraeli. She had done some reading, although not much, but did not want to regurgitate what was in the text book, which was basically hagiography.

I told her that if she wanted her essay to stand out from the pack, it would be best if she took a less prosaic approach, and she agreed. So we mapped out an essay which dealt with Disraeli's rift with Peel, his angering the party's traditional supporters, especially farmers over the Corn Laws, his only winning two terms, and his being more of a dilettante than a traditional Tory.

I left thinking the matter was well under control, but when I got to my office there was a message for me to call John's secretary, Norma Marriot, a lady for whom I had great liking and respect.

I called her back right away. "Hi Norma. What's going on?"

"Oh, Mr. Akerman!"

"Is there a problem?"

"Oh, Mr. Akerman! It's the essay."

"Did you read it? Is it okay?"

"Oh, Mr. Akerman! I think you'd better come over."

I went over and, shaking her head, Norma handed me the essay. It was incomprehensible: Every assertion made along the lines on which we had agreed, was immediately contradicted by arguments along the lines of the traditional text book stuff. Natasha had put both sides of the argument without saying, or even knowing, that there was a disputation between the two positions.

The explanation for the fiasco was forthcoming when Norma told me that John had also asked Gerry Mendelson to help Natasha with the essay, and that he had advised her to stay with the conventional narrative. So, she put both of them together without realizing that they were mutually exclusive.

It was too late to do anything about it and the essay went in as it was. It bothered me that Natasha had not told me that Gerry was also helping her, so I wondered if John had told her not to mention that.

As the years progressed it became clear that John was receiving an increasing amount of opposition to my working for him, and especially to my being publicly seen with him. I know that several deputy ministers despised me, although in some cases, like Rollie Thornhill's deputy at Development, Armand Pinard, I had no idea why as I had little or no dealings with them.

Also, various ministers had become hostile, especially Jack MacIsaac from New Glasgow, although, again, I had no idea why. When I been in the House, Jack and I had been friendly, going out to dinner and, once to a concert with Tommy Makem and Liam Clancy.

I learned that Jack's change of heart from friendship to animus was caused by his belief that, by coming to work for the premier, I had betrayed his brother Alex, who was an avid New Democrat from New Victoria in Cape Breton. It seemed like a weird reason to me, and I thought it was much more likely the result of poison being fed him by the particularly slimy and venomous sister of a member of his staff.

In any event, Jack showed his hostility in demonstrative and sometimes childish ways when Policy Board would meet.

When Carmen Moir moved from Policy Board to Community Services, the position was vacant for some time. Terry Donahoe, who was the Board's minister, said he wanted me to step into Moir's place and that he had told that to the premier.

However, it was not to be. John appointed a Tory hack, Jerry Redmond, who brought with him a bunch of whiz kids who knew nothing about government or politics and whose convoluted language was scarcely intelligible.

Knowing I could never work in such a ridiculous set-up, I could not get out of there fast enough.

So, when John called me in and asked me to do him a "great favour", I accepted with alacrity. Mavis liked the late Rev. Laird Stirling, who had assiduously attended her when she had been in hospital, so John had appointed him Minister of the Environment. However, as excellent a person as Laird was, he was given to huge flares of temper, at which times he was unable to fully control his tongue.

I was to be Laird's "Special Assistant" to help him deal with his Deputy Minister, of whom he had already made a mortal enemy, and to contain him when he got carried away by rage or enthusiasm. John adjured me never to let Laird talk to the media unless I was 100% certain he was completely calm and in control.

Laird was a lovely man, kindly, full of fun, and great company; but he had high blood pressure and loved to eat cream cakes and cookies. This made his temper more precarious, and often he would read something in the paper, then leap up roaring with rage, announcing that he was going to talk to the press and "sort out those SOBs".

When I would tell him he could not talk to the media, he would become even more enraged, shouting at me, waving his arms, and becoming bright scarlet in the face. I would stand in front of his office door and tell him that if he wanted to leave he would have to physically disable me.

After about 20-30 minutes he would calm down, his face would return to normal, and he would have a good chuckle with me. Then, as like as not, he would quietly ask if there were any squares or muffins in the office.

Telling me that he was having more trouble "from the boys", John moved me again, this time to a ridiculous job as "Special Advisor" to the Department of Sport, Recreation and Culture, where the deputy minister, Robert Geraghty, would not allow me to do anything of value. I was shunted to an office in a building a dozen blocks away.

Here, I drafted John's responses to various constituents and citizens. At least this was valuable work, in the sense it was badly needed because John's letters were brief to the point of being brusque. In reply to some earnest high school student's elaborate inquiry, John would dictate: "Dear Mr. Smith. Thank you for your letter. Sincerely, John M. Buchanan."

Norma despaired of these and seemed genuinely glad I was lending a modicum of literary flair to his correspondence.

I was languishing in this manner when I heard John saying on radio, "When the Senate train comes into the station, you get on board." He was out, and I knew my days were numbered.

I approached John's successor, Roger Bacon, about some meaningful task, as indeed I approached *his* successor, Donald Cameron, but no dice.

Then I received a visit from lawyer Michael Kontak with the news that my association with the government had been severed. He handed me papers outlining a settlement. I hired a lawyer from the most touted firm of labour lawyers in the city, but he was useless, my gaining from his exertions only an interview with a blithering fool at a so-called "head-hunting" consultancy.

For a day, I was rich, holding a cheque for the equivalent of a month's salary for each year of service, but then Percy Fleet at the Department of Finance called me saying that if I gave the cheque to him I could buy additional pension benefits when the time came.

My life with John was over.

John died, aged 88, in 2020, and his memorial service was a fitting tribute to him. Rollie Thornhill and Premier Stephen McNeil gave excellent speeches, and my friend Rodney MacDonald played a beautiful composition of his own on the violin.

16: In the wilderness

Shortly after Donald Cameron had terminated me, I was told that, when the matter had come up in cabinet, only Terry Donahoe and Tom McInnis had been in my favour, the latter, apparently, spoke most eloquently in support of my abilities and value. I shall always be grateful for that.

I was in the Legislature gallery when Richmond MLA Ritchie Mann raised the matter of my dismissal in Question Period. Premier Cameron's response was not truthful.

Not long after I left government service, I received a call from Sandy Nicholson (Peter Nicholson's nephew) informing me that he was manager of the Metro office for the Cameron newspaper chain, and that one of the papers, *The Metro Weekly*, needed an editor as its previous incumbent, Al Hollingsworth, had left to establish a brand new weekly to be called *The Patriot*. I accepted the offer and went to work in a seedy office attached to Cameron's steel company on Windmill Road in Dartmouth.

Apart from Sandy, there were three salespeople working out of the office, selling ads for a variety of papers, such as *The Vanguard*, *The Coastguard*, *The Progress-Enterprise*, and *The Advertiser*. A cold-blooded woman called Dorothy controlled the operation from the Vanguard offices in Yarmouth, under the overall leadership of R.B. Cameron Jr.

I had known Bob's father, R.B. Senior, over the years, a colourful and cantankerous buccaneer of industry who at one point had been president of the SYSCO steel plant in Sydney. I got along well with him in private (as indeed I did with his son) and have some lasting memories of him. One was when I was walking down the street in London, and I heard a noise. I looked round and there was

R.B. hanging out of a taxi window, laughing and shouting, "Chickenshit Akerman!"

Another was when, as head of Sydney Steel, he appeared before the Legislature's Industry Committee and refused to answer any of my questions, responding to each one by standing, bowing and saying, "I do my best for the province of Nova Scotia."

His son was a different person, not least because he was extraordinarily tall, and much less cranky. On the only occasion I asked for a raise, he granted it on the spot. However, it has to be said that the pay was only $20,000 per annum in the first place.

The job involved producing copy of various kinds and physically fitting it around the ads which Sandy and the others had sold. I soon found that I would have to write most of the copy. Later, when advertising started to dwindle, I had to write short stories and wine columns to fill the space. I inherited some columnists from Hollingsworth, but when I asked readers to rate them, found out that most were not even read.

I accumulated my own writers who, at first, provided their material without pay. Even when, later, I was allowed to pay them, I was not able to give any of them more than $20 per article.

Some of those who wrote for me included Harry Flemming, Alex J. Walling, David Publicover, Ron MacDonald, Charlie Phillips, an anonymous writer known as "The Observer", and the infamous Donald F. Ripley, best known for the book *Bagman: A life in Nova Scotia Politics*.

Among the extraordinary tales Ripley told me when he was hanging around the office, were that he was one-seventh Mi'kmaq (which still puzzles me), and that he was responsible for the multi-million dollar investigation and trial of former premier Gerald Regan, by telling the New Minas RCMP that Regan had raped his sister. Ripley was a megalomaniac and a terrible liar, and it was hard to know what and what not believe in the torrent of invective which came out of his mouth.

His book, and his venomous antipathy towards Regan, stemmed from Ripley having been a funds collector for the Liberal Party.

When Regan did not give him the attention and credit he thought he deserved, Ripley walked across the street and offered his services to the Conservatives. The Tories accepted his offer and he continued to be a "bagman", but now for the other side.

When I pressed him on the Regan affair, I asked on what grounds and with what evidence he had laid the information with the police. He said that he had been in the next room when his sister was allegedly raped. To which I asked why, if he had been in the "next room" as he claimed, did he not walk in and stop the "rape"? He glowered at me and exited the office.

Ripley was one of the most volatile, untrustworthy and unsavoury people I have had the misfortune to meet. He died of pneumonia in 2009, aged 75

~

The media industry was already changing before I went to the *Metro Weekly*, but by the time I was there it was in a state of advanced flux. Other media were replacing print advertising, and in a fairly small market, competing with the daily *Chronicle Herald* was becoming increasingly difficult. Al Hollingsworth's *Patriot* was dead almost before it was born and, even after a very large investment in it by Bob Cameron, it did not long survive its first few issues.

Because smaller outlets like the *Metro Weekly* could not possibly match the Herald's circulation they had to reduce their rates to secure orders, which meant that the meagre revenue no longer justified the publication's continued existence. In addition, the TV Guide, which had been the reason many readers bought the paper, became redundant because the information could be more readily accessed on cable television.

In that atmosphere, I could not have continued for long anyway, because it created a conflict between content which would attract readers and the need to sell ads. In the best newspapers, Editorial and Sales have a solid firewall between them, neither being influenced by the other; but when our sales staff formed the mistaken mindset that a controversial article would cost them business, they ganged up to try to stop various items and writers being published.

It was an unsustainable situation. So, one day, without any warning, cold-blooded Dorothy arrived in her Cadillac, seized my computer, and unceremoniously showed me the door.

~

During this period an extraordinary incident occurred which I still find improbable even though I know it really happened. Gerry Doucet and I were out at Jerry Regan's house on Shore Drive in Bedford. It was a nice warm night so, after dinner, we sat out on the deck chatting and enjoying a glass of scotch.

Doucet mentioned that the Lieutenant Governorship would soon be vacant. Jerry, always full of the devil and up for a prank, suggested we call someone, pretend to be from the prime minister's office, and ask them if they would be interested in becoming the new Lieutenant Governor. We racked our brains for a while, suggesting any number of unlikely candidates, including Arnie Patterson and Bill Gillis, until I finally thought of Jim Kinley of Lunenburg.

"Yes!!" the other two exclaimed in unison.

Because I had done some acting, and because they both claimed that Jim would recognize their voices, they insisted I make the call, so I did. In my best educated French Canadian accent, I told Jim I was François Grenier, the prime minister's appointment secretary. I said he should understand that my call did not constitute an offer *per se*, but was of an exploratory nature. The prime minister had asked me to inquire if Monsieur Kinley would accept the position if it were to be decided he were the most suitable choice. Jim said he was delighted and humbled to be considered and that I should inform Mr. Chretien than he was available if called upon.

Imagine our astonishment when some weeks later, it was announced on the news that Jim Kinley was to be the new Lieutenant Governor!

A further sequel was that I ran into Jim on the waterfront one day when I was out for my morning run, and we fell to chatting. I asked him how he enjoyed the new job and whether it came as a huge surprise to him. He said he not been surprised because he had received some warning of the appointment, but he had had a "funny feeling" about it because the man who called him then was not the same man who later confirmed his appointment!

~

In one of the Halifax Mayoralty elections, my old friend Brian Young and I volunteered to work for Art Flynn. Art was a big Liberal, and throughout the campaign I got to meet some thoroughly good people like Jack Armitage, Matty Burke, and Bill MacDonald, all of whom were active in the Liberal Party.

By that time, my attitude towards Vince MacLean, the party leader, had changed considerably since he had been a rather nasty, partisan Speaker of the House in the 1974-78 session. I met with him and he encouraged me to join, become involved and, in his pregnant words, "get on at the back of the bus."

Thereafter I was a member of the Liberal Party and an active worker for eleven years, during which time I got to know a number of very decent people, although most of them struck me as being rank amateurs when it came to practical politics, and all over the place when it came to ideology. In same room, it was possible to have a great guy like Lauchie MacLean, who believed that immigration was "what Canada is all about", and racists such as Jim Connolly had been when he was an MLA with me in the 1970-74 session of the Legislature. They talked about "Liberalism", but could not define it, and nearly all of them were Liberals because their parents had been Liberals (and their parents too). A few, like the excellent Jack Armitage and the equally worthy Charlie Baxter, had been Conservatives but they were in a distinct minority.

On the back of the membership application, it said that one had to pledge agreement with and support for the 'principles of the Liberal Party'. When I asked a member of staff to explain to me what those principles were, she looked stunned, thought for a minute, then said, "Well, it's about winning, isn't it?"

She was right. The Liberal Party, especially at the federal level, is all about getting power and keeping power, and will move to the left or right (and sometimes in both directions at the same time) at the drop of a hat if it is electorally beneficial. It is sad to relate that today the Conservative Party is little different. At one time one sensed that Tories actually believed in something, even if one didn't agree with what that was, but now they are so terrified of a corrupt media that they are often competing to be more Politically Correct than their opponents.

Judging by the performance of the one and the public utterances of the other, over the past decade in Nova Scotia, Liberal Stephen McNeil (one of the best premiers we have ever had, in my judgment) has been more fiscally conservative than the Conservatives; and, in the 2022 election in Nova Scotia, any New Democrat could have written the Conservative platform. Also, it can readily be argued that, federally, Trudeau Junior has, in some respects, been more left wing than the NDP.

Here, I am not advocating for one party or the other, but am advancing the notion that it would be better, and less confusing, if the electorate had real, meaningful choices, and the parties actually were what they say they are. When every party is, in effect, a liberal party, voter choice is entirely illusory.

In any event, while with the Liberals, I worked in several campaigns, being campaign manager twice and a candidate once. The latter came about when the New Democrat MLA for Halifax Fairview, Eileen O'Connell, died and a by-election was called in the depth of a terrible and bitter winter.

The NDP nominated lawyer Graham Steele, who was later to become a friend and who is largely responsible for my writing this book. The active Liberals (as opposed to those who show up once in a blue moon to throw their weight around) encouraged me to seek the nomination, as I knew the constituency, having managed the 1998 campaign of Bob Britten, who had racked up a respectable vote of 2,600.

I was opposed by a taxi driver, and by a doctor whose name was mentioned in awed tones. My troops were nervous because the other side, led by Derek Wells, a one-term MP for the South Shore who had no connection with or, apparently, knowledge of the constituency, had signs, banners, hoopla, cheerleaders and lots of noise.

I told my people to sit quietly through the *sturm und drang* and not to worry. I knew we had the numbers, largely thanks to the Lebanese-Canadian community and, in particular, to the excellent Diab/Metledge family.

We each gave speeches, mine extemporaneous, the doctor's read from a long script, and the crowd voted. One of my scrutineers, friend Allan Sullivan (son of a former Attorney General who had sat in the Legislature with me), told me that the taxi driver received one vote, the doctor got two, and I got all the others.

I accepted the nomination, announced Jack Armitage as my campaign manager and Lena Diab as my official agent, and we were off to the races. (Some years later, Lena became the MLA for Halifax Armdale, and a member of the cabinet. At the time of getting this book ready for the press in 2022, she is the Member of Parliament for Halifax West.)

I knew there was no way we could possibly win unless Graham dropped dead and they replaced him with the village drug dealer, but, at 59, my goals were to get myself into shape and to force Graham to work like a slave for every one of his votes. The weather was unspeakably appalling, giving us repeated ice storms during which I skidded and fell dozens of times, and heavy snowfalls requiring me to wade waist deep up the streets.

To the best of my knowledge I went to every door in the riding, to well over half I went twice, and to some three times. We had a limited number of workers, little money and, most crucially, none of our supporters owned four-wheel-drive vehicles. Bob Britten, who postured as a pious Christian and on whose behalf I had worked day and night in his election, did not even have the decency to show his face, or at least I never saw it.

I figured that if Election Day were a fine, sunny day, Graham's majority might be in the region of 1,000, but also that we would get a respectable total. In the event, the day was as foul as could be imagined, so bad indeed that on my way up Joseph Howe Drive to the headquarters that morning, my car skidded and did three full circles before straightening out.

Graham's campaign, which was much better organized than ours, did have four wheel drive vehicles and were able to drag their voters to the polls, with the result that he got more than twice as many votes as we did, garnering 2,164 to our 1021 and the Tories' 466. However, the turn-out was abysmal, fewer than 4,000 out of an eligible total of around 13,000 having voted: no more than 30% of the electorate.

Subsequently, I have teased Graham that he got elected with only 17% of the electorate, but the voters made a wise decision, as Graham was an outstanding MLA for 12 years.

~

Then came the Savage years, when the Nova Scotia Liberal Party, in opposition since 1978, finally came to power with a large, comfortable majority. Pundits and media hacks still say that Savage's downfall was the result of his 'abolishing patronage' and the party faithful rebelling against him for that reason. If it really happened that way, I never saw any hint of it, although it never made any sense to me to appoint your enemies or to hand political power to non-elected bureaucrats. It was politicians scared of making unpopular decisions that gave the Board of Public Utilities preposterous powers and decision-making over which the people have no control, or redress unless they are wealthy enough to go to court, just as the allegedly sacred cow the Charter of Rights handed extensive, unwarranted power to non-elected judges.

From what I could see, what set both party and public against John Savage had to do with his own arrogance, some inexplicable decisions, and what was seen as his health minister's rampaging through the province, closing hospitals.

As to the first, it is worth noting that I knew John socially through the Welsh Cultural Society and we got along very well. Even in such a setting as that he could be a little snooty sometimes, but in a friendly way. But when standing in front of a TV camera he became a different man entirely: then he came across as patronizing, brusque and high-handed. It was Dr. Jekyll and Mr. Hyde.

An illustration of the second was municipal amalgamation, which when out of office John had vigorously opposed, while Rollie Thornhill (both were former mayors of Dartmouth) had been in favour. After John took office, both reversed their positions.

Amalgamation in greater Halifax-Dartmouth was deeply unpopular (as I found later at the doors during the Fairview by-election). People could not see any logical reason for turning the entirety of Halifax County into one municipal governmental unit, and they certainly did not swallow the "economies of scale" argument which is always trotted out in such cases but almost never proves to be legitimate.

I could see this was going to be an enormous yoke around the government and the party's necks, so I tackled John Savage about it. He told me it was being done because the various industrial commissions which some municipalities had established were competing with each other with the result that the province was losing potential new business which could employ thousands.

If that were the case, I asked, why didn't the government just amalgamate the industrial commissions and leave the rest alone.

"You don't understand!" he snapped and walked away.

That was to be a familiar response to anyone questioning any of the government's policies or decisions: "You don't understand". When a leader says that to a sufficient number of supporters often enough, a mightily pissed-off party rank and file is the inevitable result, and many will long nurture their grievance.

On the third point, it has to be said that Ron Stewart, who was the new Health Minister, is a very likeable and agreeable man who obviously knows what he is talking about when it comes to medicine, but he was a lousy communicator, and not only did not carry the public with him, but did not seem to care if they understood what he was doing. At root, it was John's fault because, as he told me several times, he gave Ron 'free rein' to do what he thought was best.

My view is that when any premier gives any minister free rein, they both deserve everything they get. With poor public relations by the government and the usual sensational garbage from the media, the impression was created—and remains—that Stewart and Savage were dismantling the health care system and leaving us vulnerable and unprotected.

It came to a head when the party eventually held a vote of confidence. On the day, I was very active and, whilst we had no proof, I and everyone I met and/or worked with that day were totally convinced John had lost the vote: Quite literally, we had met nobody that day who said they were voting to sustain the Leader.

We were astounded when the official word was that he had won quite handily. My friend John Young, who was party president at the time, is one of the very few who knows whether or not there was any funny business at or after the count; but if the truth is at variance with the official verdict, I imagine he will take that knowledge to his grave.

~

One of the most invigorating episodes during this period of my life was in 1992, when Prime Minister Brian Mulroney (who, incidentally, was one of the better politicians I observed at federal-provincial conferences, far better than Pierre Trudeau) attempted to pass the Charlottetown Accord.

This measure sought to amend the Canadian Constitution by recognizing Quebec as a distinct society. All ten provinces supported this piece of virtue-signalling window dressing, but since everybody knew that Quebec society was "distinct"—just as were Newfoundland or Nova Scotia—many thought this a meaningless exercise and something of an insult to thinking people. The government announced there would be a referendum on October 26.

The "Yes" campaign was represented by all provincial governments, corporate Canada, the CBC, ITV, most newspapers, and just about every member of the self-appointed elite. Indeed, when the results of the referendum were coming in, the CBC news anchor several times asked their reporters in the field: "How are *we* doing?"

Their campaign was overflowing with cash and in Nova Scotia was headed by Robbie Shaw, Alexa McDonough's brother.

At first, it seemed as if the referendum would be little more than a formality. But, around a table in Halifax's Henry House over pints of ale, a few people had other ideas. They were Charlie Phillips, a mostly unemployed musician; retired university president Owen Carrigan, and myself. We vowed Robbie Shaw would not have it his own way.

When Shaw heard that we had set up the "No" committee under Charlie's leadership, he told the press something to the effect that "poor Charlie is struggling to be heard even though he has no funds and no supporters." He was right in that we had no more than a few hundred dollars between us, while his campaign had tens of thousands; but if he thought we had no supporters, he had another think coming.

In the event, the Accord was decisively rejected by the people of Canada, including those in Quebec itself and in Nova Scotia. On election night, Charlie was asked to comment. "Poor Robbie," he said. "He must have been weighed down by his money bags."

~

Eventually John Savage stepped aside and there was a leadership convention which Russell MacLellan won. He inherited, but could not keep, John's majority in the Legislature.

In the subsequent election in 1998, there was an equality of seats for the Liberals and NDP (19 each), but since Russell was the incumbent, the Lieutenant Governor asked him to form another government. It did not, could not, last long, and a year later the Tories came through the middle and won with 30 seats to 11 for each of the other parties.

Many attribute Russell's declining fortunes to the so-called 'Seven Seconds of Silence' in a televised Leaders' Debate when, completely against the rules, Tory Leader John Hamm asked Russell a direct question. Why Russell did not reply, only he knows, but according to the rules clearly laid out he was right not to do so, and it is to the CBC's eternal shame that they did not enforce their own directive and allowed the silence to continue for so long.

But the days when the CBC could be trusted to be fair and truthful have long gone: Today, they are a highly paid gang of propagandists, anti-Semites and liars, supported by the taxpayers to the tune of well over $1,200,000,000 a year, and they are utterly contemptuous of the fact that much of that money comes from millions of Canadians who are antithetical to their egregious bias and lack of respect for truth and principled journalism.

~

After 11 years, I did not renew my membership in the Liberal Party, basically because, while I had many friends there, I did not believe in much of what the party said and did. They were sliding headlong into the Political Correctness which has cursed and blighted western society for decades and has led to ever increasing lunacy being accepted as the norm and, most importantly, to a cancel culture which tears freedom of speech and expression to shreds in the name of not offending anyone. It is the new Fascism. The party was indeed fortunate when eventually they chose Stephen McNeil as leader who, at the very least, tried to put the brakes on the incessant spending/borrowing/taxing madness which all parties had been (and are again) espousing as if money grew on trees.

In the interim, of course, something I had only dreamed of when I was NDP leader actually happened: The NDP came to power in 2009 with a 10 seat majority and a sizable plurality of the popular vote (45.2%). I doubt if any of those heady with success on election night gave a thought as to whether the heavy slogging by Paul MacEwan and me in the early days had laid the groundwork for that moment. Still less do I think any of them dreamed that night that, in four years, they would be unceremoniously and ignominiously kicked out of office.

I voted for the Dexter government, partly because Maureen MacDonald was my own excellent MLA, but also because I was glad that Dexter was not implementing the whole grab bag of extremism the NDP always say they will enact. Had the government done nothing else other than land the massive federal government ship building project, they could have been handily re-elected. But Darrell fell into the age old trap of trying to please too many people, and (with the best intentions) shovelling public money to private industry when there was far from sufficient assurance of commensurate results. He also, unwisely, allowed himself to be publicly and closely associated with Nova Scotia Power, who were widely seen as the bad guys.

But worse, and even more central, was that the government's public relations were garbage, so bad indeed that they allowed the opposition parties to tell the government's story, instead of telling it themselves. Several times I mentioned this to an old friend who was Dexter's Number Two, "Nanky" Corbett, and each time he told me it was "all in hand".

If anyone doubts the ineptitude of the Dexter government's publicity advice, just watch their 2013 TV election commercials: Instead of showing Darrell in front of new construction sites (and there were dozens of them, all over the province) and places where people were pouring into work (like the dockyards), they had him lolling about in canteens or the like with people whose dialogue was neither uplifting nor convincing. It was truly pathetic: it looked like a party which wanted to lose.

And, as with the Savage government, the Dexter administration was riddled with hubris and, frequently, stupidity. Once, when I called the Finance minister's executive assistant with proof that an opposition MLA had egregiously lied in the House when attacking his minister, the idiot referred me to a department civil servant. So the lie went unchallenged and the attack stuck.

With friends like that nincompoop, they did not need enemies.

~

Between the 1970s and 2008, I had done very little painting. But I had done some travelling with my son, and when he was killed I was suddenly moved to paint both the places we had visited and those we planned to visit, which I would now have to see alone.

At first, I did only landscapes, mostly of Wales or Cape Breton, but later branched out into portraits, street scenes, and depictions of animals and birds. I have done hundreds of paintings in the intervening years, but have sold no more than fifty, and those at low prices. So, painting has not been a profitable business by any means and now, when my walls are covered and my closets bulging, I am slowing down because there seems little point in adding to the inventory of unwanted product.

Since those who would think nothing of blowing several hundred dollars on food and drink in one night do not see the value of something which, for less money, would give them pleasure for a lifetime, other artists also suffer. Nova Scotia is a small province but is brimming with excellent painters, most of whom are struggling to get by. Instead of giving a huge, wonderful platform to these artists, the Art Gallery of Nova Scotia devotes much of its space to outdated, second rate foreign art.

I have even tried giving some of my work away! When Boris Johnson was Mayor of London I offered to give him a series of paintings of ten of the bridges over the Thames but, not surprisingly, this was referred to a bureaucrat who thought I wanted to obtain pictures of bridges from them!

Similarly when I offered my portrait of Harry Flemming to the Art Gallery of Nova Scotia and then the Sports Hall of Fame, each of them replied by stating their lengthy acquisition process, stressing limited budgets. Finally, I called the late Gordie Gosse, who was Speaker of the Legislature at the time, and he was only too glad to accept it on behalf of the province.

Today, it hangs in the Howe Room of Province House and remains one of my best works.

But painting is in the blood, and you never know when inspiration will strike.

~

So as not to stupefy the reader with interminable detail, I will encapsulate here that this general period included losing my father, my son, my mother and my best friend, Harry Flemming; injuring myself, having surgery and having to stop running; and beginning an acting career, about which I have more to say in the next chapter.

17: Wooden boards and silver screen

During the years I was in politics, the job was so all-consuming there was no time for anything else, sadly not even enough for family But I had seen a number of my friends, including Dominic Larkin, Erin Murphy and Joanne Hagen, acting in the St. Mary's Dramatic Society productions.

So, shortly after I got out of politics and my evenings were free for the first time in years, I decided to become active in community theatre ("community" is a nice way of saying "amateur"). The transition was easy for me because prancing about on a stage had a lot in common with being in political life.

For the next ten years or so, I was involved with Theatre Arts Guild, Halifax Independent Theatre, Dartmouth Players and others. I am guessing I acted in at least a dozen productions and directed seven or eight. My first few appearances were small and doubtless clumsy, but soon I took to it like a duck to water

The first play in which I participated was *The Changeling*, a Jacobean tragedy by Middleton and Rowley, directed by Tony Johnstone, a wild and woolly egotist from Newcastle in the UK. I had a small role, Tomazo, whose line

> *I'll rather like a soldier die by th' sword,*
> *Than like a politician by thy poison.*

received a good laugh from the audience who knew I had been in the Legislature for the past ten years.

It was in this production that I first met Terry DeWolf, a very fine actor, but alas bedevilled by alcoholism. I saw Terry again in my second production, a play by Agatha Christie, then called *Ten Little Indians* (originally it had been *Ten Little N*******. Political Correctness dictates that today it is entitled *Then, There Were None*). Terry was Rogers the butler, and I played Dr. Armstrong (rather badly, I fear). Thereafter, Terry became a great friend who collaborated with me on many plays and we formed our own company, No Name Productions. This production also featured another man who was to become a long term friend, Hugh Corston. Each night, Hugh, who was gay, greatly relished saying his character's line: "I'm a good man in a tight place."

Some time later, I directed a rather lavish production for the Kidney Foundation at the Rebecca Cohen auditorium of *A Man For All Seasons*, in which Terry, Hugh and Dominic had major roles and in which the aforementioned Geordie, Tony, played Sir Thomas Moore, the lead. I played Cardinal Wolsey, who died fairly early on in the play, so I would sneak up into the 'Gods' and watch the rest of the play from on high. Unfortunately one night my bright red cardinal's vestments caught the eye of a reviewer and I was (rightly) excoriated for having "risen from the dead".

One of the more memorable of No Name's productions was *The Dresser* by Ronald Harwood, set during the Blitz of WWII, in which I was Sir, an aging, narcissistic actor, and Terry was my gay dresser, Norman. Later, this became an excellent movie starring Albert Finney and Tom Courtenay, and, later still, another film with Anthony Hopkins and Ian McKellen. Apparently, No Name was the first company in North America to get the rights to stage this wonderful play.

One evening, the fuse box blew and we lost all stage and auditorium lighting. Not knowing what else to do, Terry and I improvised for almost twenty minutes, inventing lines about Churchill and Hitler, damning the Blackout, cursing the German bombers, sneering at alleged contemporary actors etc., until repairs were complete and light was restored. Afterwards I asked some friends, Dr. David King and his wife, what they thought of the play. Not only did they like it, but they had not even suspected that our extemporizing in the dark had not been part of the script.

Another, gruelling and painful, production was *Who's Afraid of Virginia Woolf*, directed by Ernie McAulay and staged at Collins Court on the waterfront. I played George to Anna Cameron's Martha, not an easy task because Anna was very much a prima donna. Sometimes, when she disagreed with the director, she would stalk off and call her friend, the famous Canadian actress Kate Reid, then come back on stage hooting, "Kate agrees with me! I think we'll do it my way!"

Two other incidents, neither of them pleasant, mark this production in my memory. The first occurred when we were setting up, and I went up into the loft/attic to find something. Thinking the floor was solid wood rather than thin gyprock, I crashed through and plummeted some twenty feet to the concrete below. We were opening in a few hours so there could be no question of going to the hospital, so in excruciating pain I had to hobble and wince through three very long acts.

The other incident—the kind that produces cold sweat and panic in actors—happened at the beginning of the third act when Anna mistook her cue and replied with a line from Act One, whereupon the other actors repeated what they had already said over an hour previously. It was clear that none of them realized what had occurred, so I coughed loudly, said, "I'm going to get more Scotch," which they knew was not in the play, and left the stage.

As soon as I was out of sight, I grabbed a copy of the text, found out where we should have been, and charged back on stage calling out the correct cue. Had the situation not been corrected, the poor audience would have been in their hard seats for well over four hours.

The roles I enjoyed playing most were Aston in *The Caretaker*; Henry II in *The Lion in Winter*; Dafydd in *A Chorus of Disapproval*; and Sir Wilfrid Robarts in *Witness for the Prosecution*. The plays with which I was I most satisfied directing included *The Maids* by Jean Genet, with Sheila MacLean and Trish Yorke; *The Rehearsal* by Jean Anouilh; *The Prisoner* by Brigit Boland, with Dominic Larkin and Richard McConnell; and *Edwin* by John Mortimer.

One play in which I participated was Nova Scotia's entry into the Dominion Drama Festival, held in Winnipeg that year, *The Highland Heart in Nova Scotia*. During that production I met Rosemary Gilbert and we buddied up, so that later, when she was commissioned by CTV to do a series called *Windows*, she asked me to play leading roles in two of the episodes, *Old Friends* and *Insurance Against Death*. In the former, Fern Downey and I had to a bed scene in an unheated cabin on the Eastern Shore in the dead of winter. Brrrrrr!

Neither of these episodes was particularly worthy of a note in posterity, but they got me started in the TV and film business, which is something for which I shall always be grateful, because it led to my doing 143 shoots (as of time of writing), and meeting and working with Ed Asner, Rob Lowe, Hilary Swank, Harrison Ford, Danny Glover, Ellen Page, Liam Neeson, Brenda Fricker, James Caan, Sissy Spacek, Tom Selleck, Olympia Dukakis, Joan Plowright (Lady Olivier), Rutger Hauer, Kirk Douglas, Linda Hamilton, Mariska Hargitay, Michelle Williams, Gabriel Byrne, Rosanna Arquette, Kathy Baker, Kate Nelligan, Scott Glenn, Adrian Brody, Sam Elliott, Joanne Whalley, Corbin Bernson, Michael Moriarty, Jason Priestly, Cybil Shepherd, Colm Feore, Frances Fisher, Bruce Greenwood, Meatloaf, Bruce Davison, Valerie Bertinelli, William Russ, Nicholas Campbell, Megan Follows, David Cubit, Frances O'Connor, Henry Ian Cusick, Saul Rubinek, Kerry Fox, Donald Sumpter, Paz de la Huerta, Allison Pill, Cuba Gooding Jr., Aujenue Ellis and many others.

The skills required to act on stage and in movies are so dissimilar that it is amazing that so many can do both successfully.

On stage you have to be emotional, exaggerate your movements, project and speak at an unnatural volume; before the camera you have to internalize your feelings, make your actions small, and for the most part lower your voice to below conversational level. In fact, on the stage you must act, but in film you must never do so. If you do act, the camera will find you out and mark you as a "ham".

It is all about being *natural*, which is not the same thing as whispering or mumbling, which so many young actors seem to think these days. Not only is their approach unconvincing, but it is inconsiderate if your colleagues cannot even hear their cues. I think the best way is to *become* the character and then to act as normally and as naturally as he would.

There are a lot of puffed-up, big-feeling characters in the movie business and they are not confined to producers. Some actors—usually, but not always, second level or lower—can be monumental snots and, believe me, I have met my share of those.

But now and again you meet some big names who turn out to be fine people. Harrison Ford, Kathy Baker, Tom Selleck, Sam Elliott, Corbin Bernsen, and Joan Plowright spring to mind—all great people who became friends. Selleck in particular is special to me as I have worked with him on five or six different productions, and each time I admired and liked him more. He is a great actor and a great guy.

But two of the most special were beautiful and talented ladies of the highest order of angels. My warmest memories of both had to do with the eye-line.

The eye-line is what an actor gives another when the camera is on the latter. You look at him/her so he/she is looking in the right direction for the shot. There is often a lot of cheating going on and sometimes you are pressing your cheek against the camera lens, sometimes peering underneath the operator's elbow, sometimes balancing precariously on a ladder.

Some few actors do not require an eye-line. I am one of those because if I know who my character is and how he should be feeling, it doesn't matter to me whether I am speaking to a person or to a piece of tape stuck on the camera. Indeed, I have ingratiated myself to more than one director and Ist AD by having them leave my close-ups until the end of the day, letting the rest of the cast go home and thus saving the production a lot of money. So the first story is all the more amazing.

I was working a night shoot in perishingly cold weather. I had several scenes to do with the incomparable Sissy Spacek in the movie *Songs in Ordinary Time*. After some three hours we had finished Sissy's shots and the cameras were turning around to do mine.

By this time Sissy's teeth were chattering and she was starting to turn blue, so I quietly told my friend Rod Holcomb, the director, to put a flag (mark) on the camera and get Sissy back to her trailer before she froze to death. Sissy overheard us and angrily marched forward and snatching away the flag.

Pulling her thin, little coat around her shoulders, she said, "Jeremy was here for me. I'll be here for him!"

When we wrapped several hours later, neither of us could feel our fingers or toes. Not only that, but she invited us all into her trailer where she made hot soup for us. That's what I call a real star.

The second story concerns the shooting of a long, elaborate courtroom series of scenes in the film *The Plain Truth*, with Mariska Hargitay (star of *Law and Order SVU* and daughter of Jayne Mansfield) and my dear pal Robert Bockstael. No matter how good you might think Mariska (pronounced Marishhka) looks on *SVU*, believe me, she is ten times more beautiful in person.

Stars like Mariska get paid according to what is called a "picture deal"—they get a set sum no matter how long they work—while actors like me usually get paid on a daily rate with overtime kicking in after nine hours on set. She and I were discussing this between takes and I indicated that I was hoping for a lot of overtime as I needed the money. She grinned at me, and hours later after my shots had been done and they told me to go home, Mariska spoke up:

"No!" she said. "I can't do the scenes unless I can see Jeremy. I need Jeremy. I must have Jeremy."

There was some *sotto voce* muttering among the suits, who always want to limit spending (unless it is on them, their families and hangers-on), but they don't usually argue with someone of her stature, so I got at least another three hours' work at about $250 an hour because we were well into double time. What a sweetheart! Mariska is one of the nicest women I have ever met.

~

Occasionally, working on a movie can be a nightmare. I can recall two such occasions, the first when I played a Russian submariner on *Buried on Sunday*. I had taken care to learn my lines inside out, but when we were on set and the camera had started rolling, the director shouted "Cut!" then calmly told me to say the lines in Russian.

I was flabbergasted because all I knew of the language was "Da" and "Nyet".

Stammering, I explained my predicament, whereupon the director, unfazed, called out to a real Russian sailor, Andrei, who was on set, and instructed him to translate. He obliged, so the director said to me, "Say that."

Since I neither understood nor could remember what Andrei had said, I continued to stutter my apologies, so the director gave us five minutes during which I was to learn the lines in Russian. When we re-commenced I did my best, but I fear my panic was all too evident, as in the finished product most of my lines were cut.

The other occasion was when I was playing Charlie the announcer in *The Circuit*, a movie about car racing. Here, again, I had studiously learned the lines. But when I got to the track, Peter Werner, the director, ripped them up and threw them in the wastebasket.

"Here," he said, handing me new material. "These are better."

I broke out in a cold sweat because I knew we would be shooting the scenes in a matter of minutes.

"You won't have time to learn them, so I'll cut them up and stick them on the walls around the announcer's booth," he said.

So that is what we did. Scraps of paper were taped above, below and to the sides of the booth's window and I did my level best to read them off in the right order.

Though I say so myself, calamity led to triumph. If you watch the film, you would have no idea anything was amiss: It just looks as if Charlie has ants in his pants and is very excited about the action on the track!

~

An actor with a remarkable repertoire, with whom I was fortunate to work on a movie called *The Secret* about 25 years ago, was the legendary Kirk Douglas. We were playing political opponents running for Assemblyman in a New England state.

Two things surprised me about Kirk. One was how short he was (I later learned that the majority of movie stars are quite small people). The second was that he read every line off a huge portable teleprompter. It was first time I had seen that done, although not the last, because Ed Asner also used one when I worked with him in several seasons of Thom Fitzgerald's *Forgive Me.*

I first saw Kirk in *The Vikings* when I was a kid, and shortly thereafter in *Spartacus.* I would not say he was a very great actor, but he was certainly a wonderful performer and enormously popular entertainer.

In 2003 I was cast as the Chief Executive Officer of Kmart in *Martha Inc.,* the story of Martha Stewart, and had a number of scenes with the star, Cybil Shepherd. It was a nightmare because one never knew what to expect from a woman who was obviously out of control. Cybil had an alcohol problem for many years, eventually going into rehab for treatment. While we were shooting the movie, it seemed to me that Cybil was either hammered or well on the way to being in that condition. She missed her cues, invented lines, and was physically uncoordinated. It was all very sad, because she is a nice person and was a considerable talent.

Another actor with whom I worked on two shoots (*Dawn at Sunset* and *Emily of New Moon*), and who became a close friend for some years, was Michael Moriarty, former star of *Law and Order.* He was highly intelligent, widely read, greatly talented (as a composer and musician as well as an actor), and had won a Fulbright scholarship to Oxford when he was young.

I have not found an official version of the event, but Michael once told me that he had to be taken back from Florence to England via hospital plane because he had collapsed in either the church of Santa Maria de Fiore or Santa Maria Maggiore (I forget which) because he had seen Christ. Sober, he was the best and most agreeable company it would be possible to find; intoxicated he was insufferable: querulous, paranoiac, accusatory and foul-mouthed. At dinner with him it was possible to see, with each glass of wine he drank, a gradual physical transformation from a friendly, benevolent Dr. Jekyll to an ugly, snarling Mr. Hyde.

He had a notion that the Clinton administration in the USA was out to get him (according to him, they were also targeting Angela Lansbury), and he said the CIA was spying on him at the orders of Attorney General Janet Reno. Once, when he was renting an apartment on Barrington Street in Halifax, Nova Scotia, he conceived the idea that the Agency was installed in an office on the opposite side of the street directly across from him.

"Look," he said to me earnestly one day, "See that? That's the camera. They're filming me day and night."

I thought this was crazy, so I went across the street, climbed the stairs and looked into the office concerned. What Michael thought was a camera was in fact an old-fashioned slide projector; but when I told him that, he was not convinced I was telling the truth.

Michael had met Suzanna Cabrita when he was in Halifax. She was and is a fine lady, but their relationship was marred by Michael's drinking and paranoia, and I believe their marriage lasted only a year.

Their wedding was like something out of a farce. For days prior to the ceremony, Michael was incommunicado (drinking continuously in a hotel) and we were not sure if he would even show up at the chapel. In the event, he did make it there, but was clearly inebriated, at one point falling on his knees at the altar. The banquet following the wedding was equally bizarre, and subsequent to the dinner he sprayed the white silk walls of the bridal suite with red wine.

One of the greatest personal tragedies I have ever known was this lovely, bright guy blighting his own life and the lives of those around him. I have not seen him for some years, but I understand he has married again and lives in British Columbia.

The last contact I had with him was when he was furious with me because I refused to agree that Dvorak was the greatest composer who ever lived. I said it was matter of personal taste, but Michael would not accept that and excoriated me for being an ignorant fool. I decided that was a good juncture at which to not to poke the bear and to leave well enough alone.

However, I most earnestly hope he is both healthy and happy now.

~

I think my most enjoyable film shoots were Thom Fitzgerald's TV series *Forgive Me;* the feature *Virginia's Run,* directed by Peter Markle; and *The River Man,* directed by Bill Eagles. In the first, I was one of four priests living together in a rectory until, in the final season, only two of us, Mike Macleod and I, were left. This was because my dear old friend John Dunsworth had unexpectedly died, which elevated me to the Number Two role and gave me many more scenes and some memorable one-on-one encounters with Mike's character: I think it is some of my best work.

In *Virginia's Run* I was a stuffy English nincompoop who eventually gets thrown into a pond by local townspeople. It was great fun, and I got to meet Joanne Whalley and spend time with Gabriel Byrne.

In the *River Man*, I played Detective Lieutenant Downing and got to wear a mean-looking gun along with its shoulder holster.

These are among my favourites, chiefly, I think, because these are my favourite directors. Many, if not most, directors feel compelled to give you instructions even when they know, and know that you know, they are redundant or repetitive.

Once, I had a scene with Danny Glover in which we sat at a kitchen table and talked. Before rolling, the director conspiratorially took me aside and in a low voice said, "So, you're sitting at the table with Danny. And you're, you know, talking to each other.

Think you can do that?"

I said I thought I could do that, so I sat at the table and talked to Danny.

Directors are quite within their rights to do that sort of thing, but the ones who get the best work out of actors are those who speak to you only when necessary.

The best example of this was on *River Man*, when Bruce Greenwood, Cary Elwes, Sam Jaeger and I sat down with director Bill Eagles to do a read-through of the script. As we went along, Bill continually gave Bruce, Cary, and Sam a multitude of advice and instructions, but said not one word to me. Afterwards I caught up with Bill in the hallway and asked why he was, in effect, discriminating against me.

I shall treasure his reply forever, "Jeremy, you'll hear from me when you do something wrong."

Thom Fitzgerald is like that. Apart from pleasantries or jokes between set-ups, he does not waste words. As long as you don't hear from him, you know you are on the right track. That approach makes it an additional pleasure to work with such a talented and likeable man.

Also, his partner, Doug Pettigrew is my favourite producer because he is so kind and considerate, always anxious to help and make life easier for cast and crew. I would rather work with Thom and Doug than George Lucas, Stephen Spielberg and all the stars in Hollywood.

I am also very fond of Robert Harmon, who has directed me five or six times in various *Jesse Stone* movies and in *November Christmas;* and Karen Arthur (famous for directing *Cagney and Lacey*), with whom I have worked on *The Secret* and on *Passion and Prejudice*.

I also greatly enjoyed playing Lamar, the sinister Chief of Staff to the prime minister in the series *Snakes and Ladders*, directed and filmed in an eccentric and, I think, unsuccessful way by Sturla Gunnarsson, who had cameras hanging on belts instead of fixed on dollies or tripods. The constant swirling and drifting of the images often made one feel as if one had travel sickness.

~

Inexperienced actors and the general public tend to think that it is much better to work on an expensive, blockbuster Hollywood movie than on a small-budget production, but nothing could be further from the truth. I have worked a few of the former, like *K-19, The Widowmaker* and *Amelia*, but, in my experience, the bigger they are the tougher the work, the worse the conditions, and the greater the dangers.

On *Amelia*, for example, dozens of actors and extras were left out in the cold rain for hours on end, and the portable toilet was a ten minute walk away. On *Chapelwaite* (a big budget series based on a Stephen King novel), we worked outside at night in sub-zero temperatures, often in cramped and/or dusty and dirty conditions; and at age 78 I had to run like a hare over rough, uneven ground, roll around in the dirt, and do boisterous fight scenes.

I am not complaining because the money was obscenely good, but am illustrating the point that bigger is not better when it comes to personal comfort and safety.

K-19 was an enormous production (the producer told me it was well over $100 million US in 2002) which was shot in various locations around the world, and starred Harrison Ford and Liam Neeson. My involvement in the picture came as a complete surprise, out of the blue, when I got a call from the late Gilles Belanger asking me if I was busy.

I said "No," whereupon he said that a car would pick me up outside in ten minutes.

I had no idea what this was all about, but went downstairs and climbed in. I asked the driver where we were going, to which he grunted, "The wharf."

When we got to the harbour, a man came towards me and said, "Get in the Zodiac."

By this time I was feeling like the character in *Frantic* or one of the Cary Grant movies, but I got in and we headed out to sea. After a while, when an enormous submarine bearing a red star loomed out of the haze, I finally caught on that this escapade had to do with *K-19*, which I had heard was filming off our coast.

A perilous-looking rope ladder was flung down the side and, still in my dress shoes, I clambered to the top and grabbed the outstretched hand.

"Welcome aboard, Jeremy," Liam Neeson said as he pulled me up.

He took me to meet Harrison Ford, who was equally as friendly and welcoming, and they introduced me to my dialect coach, saying I should go with him and learn how to speak with a Russian accent.

I thanked them but said I had no idea why I was there. They explained to me that the role of Captain Fyodor Tsetkov, the captain of the submarine which rescues the K-19 when it runs into nuclear trouble, was originally intended to be played by a British friend of Liam's, but the movie had reached its limit of non-Canadian actors (a matter of tax credits), so they had asked Gilles to find a Canadian substitute.

I also met the charming director, Kathryn Bigelow, and then went off to sit on the heads, where the coach taught me to speak with my tongue flattened against the back of my upper teeth. He also gave me my sides (lines) for the scenes.

The next day I was kitted out in a scratchy, ill-fitting costume (they almost always are very uncomfortable because the wardrobe people themselves never have to wear them), then went in the Zodiac with Harrison and Liam out to the submarines. As Liam carried on an endless chat with me about Ireland and about other actors, Harrison was furiously telling him to shut up, and was hurriedly crossing out all my lines and scribbling in new ones.

Since I had stayed up very late learning the original lines, this did not make my job any easier.

At sea, the shoot centred on two Russian submarines, one large one, the K-19, which was about 370 feet long, weighing something like 5,000 tons. The other was less than half the size. The first was

Harrison's vessel, the second was mine.

The two subs rode side by side, about 20 feet apart, connected by thick hawsers. As the sea swelled, the subs would roll apart to the limit of the hawsers, then come rolling back together with a frighteningly loud thump.

Conditions aboard my vessel were appalling, and exceedingly dangerous. The deck may have been about twelve feet wide, yet had as many as fifty men huddled in the space with no deck rails of any kind, which meant that one false move and it would be "man overboard".

Kathryn would casually direct me to "walk up the deck" from one end to the other, but as it was so congested I could only do that with my toes gripping the very edge while grabbing, hand over hand, on to the sailors' shoulders. To add insult to terror, the heads were chained shut so people had to urinate and defecate from the edge of the deck.

My sub was supposed to be rescuing Harrison and his crew from the K-19, whose nuclear reactor was leaking, so the men had to wait for the roll to bring the vessels close to each other, and then jump from one to the other. Had the timing not been perfect, and had a man fallen, it was more than likely he would have been crushed when the ships rolled back together.

I could see fear in the eyes of many who did the jump, but Harrison did it several times. When I tackled him about this, there was an exchange which I found both hilarious and eye-opening:

"Why are you taking such a risk? If you slipped, the whole movie could be down the toilet."

"It's good for morale," Harrison said. "Good for the guys to see me do it."

"I think it's crazy."

"So, you wouldn't do it, Jeremy?"

"No way!"

"Would you do it if you were getting paid what I am?"

"How much are you getting paid?"

"$21 million."

"Ah," I said, "in that case, yes."

"Fucking right you would!" Harrison said with a big grin.

The aftermath of this was that I came close, but not nearly close enough, to having Harrison take a screenplay about the 1917 Halifax Explosion which my son and I had written (this was years before the Donovan brothers' *Shattered City* appeared). The part we had written which would have been perfect for Harrison was that of Francis Mackey, the harbour pilot at the centre of the action.

I gave the screenplay to Harrison, and he took it back with him. Soon I heard from his manager, telling me that Harrison was interested, but that they had a firm policy that they would only allow Harrison to consider screenplays which came to them from one of an approved list of Hollywood literary agencies.

I sent the script to each one on the list, but they all said they had a firm policy that they could not consider any script which did not come from one of their already "established" writers. There was absolutely no way around such ridiculous obstacles.

There have been numerous incidents on film shoots which were amusing (such as the child star loudly farting at the suspenseful moment in a crucial scene), but just two more of these anecdotes must suffice. Both concern an absolute stinker of a Disney movie called *Bailey's Mistake,* the cast of which included Joan Plowright, Kyle Secor, and Paz de la Huerta.

I was standing in line at the canteen when a tiny, skinny, rather plain-looking woman who was standing ahead of me turned around and started a conversation. We got along like a house on fire (as Dad used to say), took our food to a table and chatted for some time then went outside. A set car drew up, the driver opened the door and she got in.

I made to follow, but the driver said, "This is not for you, Jeremy."

Whereupon the woman said, "That's okay, Freddie, we're old friends."

I climbed in and she said, "I didn't introduce myself. I'm Linda Hamilton."

Another example of my not recognizing a star was when I worked with Jason Priestly on *Love and Death on Long Island.* I had a scene where, as a priest, I had to announce that a person had passed away. After we had shot it, this handsome young man and I drifted out to have a smoke (which I did in those days).

No sooner had we lit up than scores of teeny boppers engulfed us, screaming and shouting. They were not there for me, so I stepped aside.

When the young man had finished handing out autographs and they had dispersed, I asked him, "Should I know who you are?"

He replied, "Oh, man, *Beverly Hills 90210.*"

"What's that?" I asked in my ignorance.

"Oh, fuck, man," he said, "I'm a star!"

We had a good laugh over that.

Subsequently we worked together on several other shoots and each time I would greet him with, "Should I know who you are?"

~

A delicious incident occurred which illustrates a legendary jealous rivalry in the acting world. I spent a lot of time with, and became very chummy with, the magnificent Joan Plowright, who is lovely and kind when calm, but when riled like a ship of the line in full steam. Joan, who was married to the great Laurence Olivier for 28 years (which makes her Baroness Lady Olivier), and whose career spanned seven decades, was then 71 (she is still with us at 92), and would ask me to pick up the British Sunday newspapers from Atlantic News when I went back to Halifax from where we were shooting.

One day she was sitting on the edge of the woods like a *grande dame* surveying her domain when I brought the papers.

"Joan I have bad news for you. Gielgud is dead."

"Awww. That's sad. What do they say about him?"

"I'll read it to you," I said, and did so. But when I came to this passage, her manner changed: "Many say he was the greatest actor of his generation."

"Harrumph!" Joan snorted, and stalked off into the trees.

I understood. She was right to feel miffed. Sir John Gielgud was one of my greatest favourites, and one of the finest actors who ever lived, but he was not on the same level as her Larry.

~

My anecdote about Linda Hamilton is pertinent to the claim some movie people make about the camera having a biased mind of its own, which leads it to discriminate in favour of some actors and against others. The person in the street may think that is just nonsense spouted by less successful actors, but it is true.

Rarely, as in the case of Mariska Hargitay, does the camera make anyone look worse than they do in life, but for some fortunate few it is miraculously transformational. Linda is one of those; so is Hillary Swank.

When I met and worked with Hilary, she was extremely kind and friendly but looked plain and goofy, with a mouthful of huge teeth. I knew she had enormous talent, but I still wondered about her success, since Tinsel Town was notorious for judging by appearances.

So, I casually wandered behind the camera and, breaking all protocols, took a quick peek. It was amazing: through the lens, Hilary looked like Miss World.

But then, almost everything about the film world is one form of deception or another. And, increasingly, it is also about self-deception, as Hollywood generally, and many actors as individuals, have acquired megalomaniacal, narcissistic notions of their own powers, function, opinions and influence.

18: Rating the politicians and stars

Willy Brandt

Willy Brandt (whose real name was Herbert Ernst Karl Frahm) was a political leader in West Germany from the 1950s to 1974. He was Mayor of Berlin, Minister of Foreign Affairs and finally Chancellor from 1969 to 1974. In 1978, he chaired sessions of a convention in Vancouver which I attended. Despite his reputation as a freedom fighter and a swashbuckler, I found him sour and autocratic. He pretended not to see any delegate whose opinion he suspected he would not like, and when that did not work would try to bully and gavel down the speaker.

When a poor Greek man from Cyprus pleaded with the convention not to adopt a resolution admitting the Turkish delegation, describing how his wife and daughters had been raped and his house burned down by the Turks, Brandt hammered him down and, without even testing the meeting, declared the motion carried. I was temporarily leading the Canadian delegation so I leapt to my feet shouting a protest, and as I did so, another man some feet away to my left was also on his feet loudly complaining. He turned out to be Bob Hawke, a most likeable fellow who, five years later, became the most popular Prime Minister Australia ever had. We were summarily dismissed by the Chair.

After a while, I got up to go to the washroom, and as I walked up the aisle I noticed four blond, athletic giants had also risen. And I noticed that Brandt had left the Chair and was also heading out, the blond giants closing in behind him. Thinking nothing of it, I wandered out and went to the washroom. When I opened the door and walked in, I was immediately and roughly pinned to the wall by two of the blond giants who held me there while I watched

Willy Brandt take a pee. Without saying a word, or in any way acknowledging my presence, Brandt shook himself, washed his hands, and walked straight past me, whereupon the blond giants released me.

Ed Broadbent

In the 1971 NDP federal leadership race, I supported and worked hard for Ed Broadbent, but the more I got to know him, the more I realized what a terrible mistake that had been. I did not then have as much experience as I later gained of the intolerance, arrogance, and fluffy, so-called "conceptual thinking" of many university professors. Had I done so, I would have kept well clear of Professor Broadbent. As time progressed, I found his thinking antithetical to mine on tactics and goals (he wallowed in European notions of being part of coalitions). I also found him invariably snide or sarcastic on a personal level. To his considerable credit, he took the party to what I believe was its highest point to date in the 1988 election when the NDP won more than 40 seats. But overall, I found him to be extremely vain, bombastic and full of hot air.

Garnet Brown

Anyone who did not like Garnet Brown (Nova Scotia MLA, 1969-78) must have been a fool. He was among the friendliest, most warm-hearted and generous men who ever lived. He may have had his weaknesses as a public speaker (who can forget the words he created like "insinuendo"?) and as a minister, but as a human being few surpassed him. He was a partisan, to be sure, but political considerations never limited his personal kindness and generosity. Once he called me over to his car, opened the trunk and handed me an enormous, freshly-caught salmon. When I was running in a by-election in 2001, he contributed to my campaign over and over again. Paul MacEwan, who was incessantly looking for money—whether loans or handouts—never failed to benefit from Garnet's bounty. Indeed, once when Garnet was under attack on the floor of the Legislature, Paul leapt to his defence, telling the House that on the weekend he had been "strapped" but had gone to Garnet who had "fixed him up". I think it safe to say that all who knew him were better off for that fact.

Guy Brown

Like almost everybody else who knew him, I liked Guy (Nova Scotia MLA, 1974-98) very much. He was fun and good company and cultivated an "Aww shucks", country bumpkin persona which most found endearing and, more importantly, non-threatening. He was almost a god in the Liberal Party because he could give great, rabble-rousing, roof-raising, barn-burning harangues which got the troops hollering on their feet. And in his constituency of Cumberland Centre he was revered because of his relentlessly hard work on "cases" for individuals, all of which was highly commendable. But I cannot recall any significant achievements of his as a minister, nor any speech which was really thought-out, coherent and highly articulate. And, although he hid it well, he was extremely vain. In Russell MacLellan's final election as premier, when a mass rally was held in Dartmouth so he could make an announcement which was thought might turn the tide and save the government, Guy had the crowd in the palm of his hand. But rather than use that to boost the premier's announcement, he ranted and raved and rambled on well past the press deadline, thereby ensuring that maximum publicity was denied to the party's last chance. He had been in politics a long time, and I cannot persuade myself he was unaware of what he was doing.

The Donahoes

Until 1978, my knowledge of this extraordinary Nova Scotia political dynasty was confined to reading in the papers and seeing from the Legislature gallery Richard Donahoe, who was Attorney General and Minister of Health in the Stanfield and Smith governments. To me, he seemed larger than life and harshly belligerent (later, when I met him, I was amazed at how short, and how likeable, he was). According to my mindset at the time, I took him for a reactionary, almost Dickensian, Gradgrind-like figure. So convinced of this was I that in my maiden speech to the Legislature in 1970, I referred to him as "one of the greatest legal minds of the nineteenth century".

My opinion was already changing by 1978, when Richard's sons, Arthur and Terry, were elected to the Legislature. Both of them were soon to distinguish themselves in various ways. It would have been difficult to find a pair of brothers who were as engaging and agreeable, and over the years they became some of my most favourite people.

Arthur, the elder, is a thoughtful, intelligent, widely read, amusing man who is excellent company. He was an MLA for 15 years, a first class Speaker of the House for 10 years, and brought great distinction to Nova Scotia by being selected, out of hundreds of applicants around the world, as the Secretary General of the Commonwealth Parliamentary Association. In recent years, although we have had occasional minor differences, Arthur has been a firm friend and a staunch supporter of and participant in, XMLAS, the Association of Former Members of the Nova Scotia Legislature, of which I am founder and president.

When I was Number Two at the government's Policy Board, Terry Donahoe became the minister responsible, which was a most welcome development for me. When the Deputy Minister, Carmen Moir, was moved out and I became his acting replacement, I was almost ecstatic to be working directly with Terry on a daily basis. It is not easy for someone with an ego like mine to admit to harbouring even a smidgen of hero worship, but I had both enormous respect and tremendous liking for Terry, and thought we made a truly excellent team. We were on the same wavelength and never had a cross word, although I used to tease him for his prolixity and procrastination. I used to call him "Old Tomorrow" because he loved to delay decisions, and would tell him that he never used one word where ten could be employed. It is hardly an exaggeration to say that when Premier Buchanan cut this arrangement short, I was almost heartbroken.

Terry was an MLA for almost 20 years, and when Donald

Cameron boorishly quit on election night in 1993, Terry became interim Leader of the Opposition, a role at which he acquitted himself with dignity and distinction.

There were two subsequent events which raised Terry even higher in my estimation. The first was when, as Leader of the Opposition, he publicly admitted that it had been wrong to run up so much debt during the Buchanan years and that he regretted his complicity in that mistake. It is not often we see such candour in politicians, especially not when it is to their own detriment, and it was the mark of the man that he had the courage to level with Nova Scotians.

The other event was the tragic suicide of his brother-in-law, Family Court judge Paul Niedermeyer, which was the culmination of a sequence of bizarre and unsavoury episodes the details of which are best buried forever. I was deeply involved in a relationship with a family member at the time, so I was daily apprised of the details of how Terry nobly stepped up, took command, and held the family together through what must have been a hellish time. My admiration for him was unlimited.

Tragically, Terry died in 2005 at the age of 61. I kept away from all events associated with his death because, quite simply, I did not want people to see me crying.

Tommy Douglas

Tommy was not just a great spell-binding orator (I do a pretty fair impersonation of his speaking), a first rate, highly competent administrator as Premier of Saskatchewan for 17 years, and a magnificently able debater, but was also a lovely guy, full of fun and fascinating conversation. Whilst many people in the party loved Tommy as a matter of course, they found him reserved and sombre in private discourse; but that was never my experience. He could always be relied upon for a dry or pithy comment which he would just drop like a pearl for those who were attentive—like his comment that the difference between a cactus and a caucus was that with the cactus the all the pricks were on the outside.

Tommy was not only an extremely bright man, but an honest

one who knew that both Fascists and Communists sprang from the Left, and that it fell to people like him (whose political ideology devolved from the Sermon on the Mount, not Karl Marx) to find the difficult path of delivering fairness, and opportunity to ordinary people while simultaneously preserving their freedom.

Having known him as well as I did, I am confident he would not even recognize the party he founded 60 years ago. His party was all about getting a fair shake for working people and the poor. For many it is difficult to know what it is all about today, but race-baiting, political correctness, totalitarianism, pro Islamism, de-platforming and anti-Semitism all seem to be evident in alarming if varying quantities.

John Dunsworth

There are, I confess, a few women in the film/theatre industry who claim that John Dunsworth acted "inappropriately" towards them, but all such accusations are of the he said/she said variety. I cannot say if it is true, but John certainly had a ribald nature and was a fund of dirty jokes with which he would regale any who would listen.

With that proviso, I cannot think of anyone in the acting world who was more popular and more respected, and when he suddenly and mysteriously died in 2017 at the age of 71 it was an enormous shock to all of us.

John was a remarkable man, a phenomenon, who was just at home in Lapland in a Santa Claus contest as he was single-handedly building his own theatre on the seashore. He played dozens of film roles and even more in theatre, but I guess he will be best remembered as the drunken Mr. Lahey in "The Trailer Park Boys".

John and I acted in dozens of the same movies, but we did not actually appear in the same scenes until "Pit Pony" in the 1990s, and then not again until we did the "Forgive Me" series with Thom Fitzgerald. John was a delight to work with not only because he made himself heard (unlike many younger actors), but because between takes and set-ups he would tell me jokes and get me to sing numbers from Hollywood musicals. Later, in series 3 of "Forgive Me", after John's death, Thom gave my character, Father Gene, lines about singing such numbers with a fellow priest who had committed suicide. It was inspired, and a great tribute to John.

Like the rest of us, John must have had bad days when he was depressed or dissatisfied, but he never showed it. He was always upbeat, encouraging and full of fun. I miss him more with each passing year.

My tribute to John, a portrait, hangs in the ACTRA Maritimes office.

Thom Fitzgerald

I have described why I admire and like working in movies with Thom so much, but he deserves a special mention here. While others—with far less talent and ability—have moved on to greener pastures, Thom (a New Yorker originally) has stuck with Nova Scotia through thick and thin, and has continued to produce quality films and TV series right here when he could have earned infinitely more money and prestige as a writer or director in California. And, while some other producers who do continue to operate here have flooded their productions with actors from the US, New York and Toronto, Thom has done his level best to cast his productions with local actors. With the exception of the occasional star from "away", Thom's products are filled with Nova Scotia residents, many of whom he has discovered and/or developed into accomplished actors.

ACTRA, the film actors' union, makes regular awards to actors whom they think have excelled. I think it is high time they made a special award to Thom and Doug Pettigrew for all they have done for the union's membership. They owe them a huge debt of gratitude.

Michael Foot

Ever since childhood I had been hearing about Michael Foot, the wild man of the Labour left, a donnish intellectual adored by miners and radical unions, feared by his own party leadership and loathed by Tories and the ruling classes. It was not until Foot's completed biography of Aneurin Bevan came out in 1973 that I established contact with him. Bevan, a former coal miner, was a fiery orator, as well known in South Wales as Churchill or the Queen.

When I had finished reading the book, a work of considerable historical scholarship, I wrote to Michael in care of the House of Commons. The Labour Party was then in opposition, having been defeated by Edward Heath's Tories three years earlier. So when Michael replied to my letter and invited me to meet him at Westminster, it was not in the spacious ministerial office where we later met, but in Annie's Bar. Instantly we hit it off and became fast friends, despite our many and significant differences in political philosophy.

If you took what Michael said at face value, you would have to conclude he was extremely left wing and had some odd beliefs, such as that coal miners could do no wrong, whatever they might do. Whilst I thought this strange because, like his, mine was a coal mining constituency, I found this extraordinarily endearing.

After Harold Wilson was returned as Prime Minister in the election of 1974, Michael was sworn in as Secretary of State for Employment. Over the next few years I saw him frequently and our friendship grew. When, in 1976, Wilson stepped down and was succeeded by Jim Callaghan, Michael was named Deputy Prime Minister and Leader of the House of Commons.

On several occasions, I took my son or my brother to lunch or dinner with Michael in the parliamentary restaurant. My son, then quite small, was thrilled when Michael took us to the Gay Hussar in Soho and talked the owner into letting Gareth run riot in the kitchen and then choose any number of items from the menu. One of his choices was roast Michaelmas goose with creamed red cabbage.

It was in the winter of 1979, dubbed "The Winter of Discontent" by the media, that I saw Michael at his best and worst. The government was under siege. Millions of union members were on strike, gasoline was hard to find, trains and buses had stopped running, garbage piled up in the streets and corpses remained unburied.

While it became clear that it was Michael, rather than Jim, who was holding the government and the party together, it was equally clear (as I have mentioned in an earlier chapter) that the country was, in effect, being run by Moss Evans, General Secretary of the Transport and General Workers Union, which represented most of the workers out on strike. Watching Michael use his charm and extraordinary fixing abilities in meeting after meeting, mollifying and unifying, filled me with admiration. Less inspiring was his apparent belief that there was nothing the government could or should do to end the strike.

Michael was a tremendous orator, both in meetings and on the floor of the Commons, passionate, polished and eloquent. He was always in a scrap with someone or other, whether in his own ranks, with Mrs. Thatcher or with the media. Whatever else you might say of him, you could never describe Michael as being dull or lacking colour.

One day he and I were walking along the street on our way from the House of Commons to Smith Square when, on the other side, a portly, red-faced man, wearing a three-pieced, pin striped suit and wielding a gold-topped cane approached. The man furiously shook his cane at us, shouting, "Communist! Bloody Communist!"

Whereupon Michael shook his cane at the man, shouting, "Fascist! Bloody Fascist!"

After we had walked on a little I asked, "Who was your friend?"

Michael peered at me through his thick, bottle glasses. "Never seen him before," he said, "but it happens to me all the time."'

Michael has been dead these 11 years and I am glad he did not live to see the utter travesty his party and movement have become. From a pro-Israel, working people's party, with as many as 20 Jewish MPs at one time, the Labour Party has turned into an anti-Semitic, fascist rabble which embraces terrorists, uses bully-boy tactics to suppress unwanted opinions, and holds ordinary people in contempt

John Hamm

I do not know John Hamm well, having met him in person only two or three times, but I have been impressed by his serious regard for his province and for his apparent probity. His record as premier is, I think, a good one, particularly in fiscal matters. For me, his low point was when he sent cheques to Nova Scotians as an election bribe, something of which I am sure he is not overly proud. I think our province is the better for John having served us, and person-ally I am grateful for the support he has given me as President of XMLAS, the Association of Former Members of the Nova Scotia Le-gislature.

Burnley "Rocky" Jones

There is an old story about people at a funeral hearing the eulogy, then going to check the coffin to make sure the priest was talking about the right person. I am in that position relative to the le-gendary, heroic stature to which Rocky Jones has been raised by the media, leftists and the race industry. I knew Burnley for many years, and the person who was my friend bears no resemblance to the hagiographic depiction of him related with bated breath by all and sundry.

The only consciously racist act I am aware of having performed was to hire Burnley as my Legislative Assistant. Put simply, I hired him because he was black, which was quite wrong, just as wrong as it would have been to hire someone because they were Caucasian or Asian. It was also a mistake, because he was useless at the job, spending most of his days with his feet up on the desk, phoning the multitude of women he had all over the city. He could be good company, but I never found him to be especially intelli-gent, original, or politically insightful. By comparison, his remark-able wife Joan, with whom I had a personal relationship after they were separated, was head and shoulders above him in intellect and understanding.

What Burnley was exceptionally good at was attracting personal publicity, at self-aggrandisement and at obtaining special treatment wherever it was available. He readily adopted whatever mantle was fashionable in the race community, from Black Panther in the 1960s and early 70s to senior statesmen of the Civil Rights movement later on. I do not suggest that Burnley never helped people or did not fight needed battles; but from my observations, whenever he did so, he made sure it was always about himself, too.

David Lewis

For some years, David, national NDP leader from 1971 to 1975, treated me with disdain and deliberate disfavour, siding with my enemies in Nova Scotia, after he learned that I had (I admit, mistakenly) supported Ed Broadbent in the 1971 election which elevated David to the party leadership; but later I became quite friendly with him and his lovely wife Sophie. He was certainly a fascinating man, but not an easy one. When he was not on guard, alert for traps, and being careful not to reveal his hand, he was often preening. He particularly loved to boast of his ability to speak French, and on one occasion when he was in full flight at a party Council meeting, he made a massive Freudian slip, saying: "I have been the centre of this party for decades." He most certainly had been *at* the centre, but I have no doubt he really believed he *was* its centre.

Unlike Tommy Douglas, who if he saw a solution to a problem on the other side of a wall, might try to bash his way through the bricks, David would peer over, and around, test the mortar and, if he thought success unlikely would back off. This gave him the reputation of being on the so-called "right" of the party, an establishment figure who was ideologically timid. I never bought this. There are few who will agree me, but I believe David Lewis was secretly an out-and-out Communist who adapted his speech and methodology according to what he thought was possible or practical in any particular circumstance. Given the power, I think David would have been a ruthless and intolerant despot. His role in the Stalinist-like expulsion of Paul MacEwan from the NDP in 1980 only reinforced this view. It was his lowest moment and I lost all respect I had had for him.

James "Buddy" MacEachern

When Paul MacEwan and I determined we had to beat Mike Laffin in Cape Breton Centre in the 1974 election, we had no idea who our candidate would or should be. One day, we pulled in for burgers at the McDonalds located at the edge of the town of New Waterford. While we were sitting there, a fellow in coveralls and loaded with frozen meat patties came up to the car and introduced himself, saying he wanted to get involved with the NDP and would like to be a candidate.

We had nobody else on the horizon and, knowing that with enough time, enough planning, enough organization and hard work, almost anyone could get elected at least once, we encouraged Buddy to get on board and start digging in.

He did as we instructed, following our plan to the letter, with the result that he was elected twice to the House of Assembly. The first time, 1974, his majority was 637 votes, so the popular conclusion that he had put his campaign over the top by bedding every women in the senior citizens units seems unlikely; but when in 1981 he lost by 464 votes, it led a former premier to say, "Buddy fucked his way into office, then fucked his way out again."

Apart from wanting to be an MLA and, if possible, *stay* an MLA, Buddy's preoccupation, his overriding obsession in life, was to copulate with as many women as he possibly could, and he did not in the slightest care what they looked like, how old they were or what their mental capacity was. One night, he reeled off all those he could remember, but fell asleep at the count of 147. He boasted of having had sex with any number of women known to me (including, he claimed, Alexa McDonough), and at an NDP national convention would spend all his time attempting to secure a conquest from every province and territory.

"Boss," he used to tell me seriously, "You must try to get every woman you meet, and be prepared to fail. Otherwise, you'll get very little pussy in life."

The tactic he used—with astounding, appalling success—was

what he called "Little Boy Lost". He would talk about having contracted "silicolosis" in the pit, having got his half his Grade 12 (Grade 6) and having learned new words like "cardboard box" and "station wagon". He would also tell strange women that they "would be so easy to love" and say to women in bars that he was sure he had seen them on television. The grotesqueness of his audacity was, sad to say, matched by the astonishing gullibility of his targets.

Buddy's obsession occasionally led him into perilous territory. Late one night he phoned me from a hotel room where he had taken a woman he had met in a bar. He was bleeding from the scrotum, he told, me and wondered if he should be worried. I said he should be worried and, unless he had a ready explanation for the discharge, he should go to the hospital. He replied by asking me if the bleeding could be caused by his sexual exertions having torn apart the sutures of the vasectomy he had received earlier that day!

From complaints I received (including one which, hilariously, said: "I have no thrust in Mr. MacEachern"), I gathered that Buddy was not that diligent with constituency case work. In the Legislature, his speeches were ill (if at all) researched and were aimed to get cheap laughs. In this category were his attacks on the government, in which he likened each minister to a fruit or vegetable; and one, very close to the wind, when he compared a minister with British Liberal Leader Jeremy Thorpe (a bisexual), saying he spent time on his knees and was "trying to get in by the back door."

Buddy was good and lively company, but he was an inveterate and often vicious gossip. I should have known at the time that, if he were denigratingly sniping to me about Paul MacEwan, Len Arsenault and others, there was a high probability he was doing likewise about me to them. He was indeed and, as described in a previous chapter, he was involved in highly questionable activities behind my back.

Paul MacEwan

Elsewhere in this book, I have discussed people who displayed Dr.

Jekyll and Mr. Hyde characteristics of a split personality, but I often thought Paul MacEwan had multiple personalities, many of them in conflict, if not at war, with the others. This, to some extent, was reflected in his private life wherein, for years, he had a home in Whitney Pier with his wife Carol, and another with a woman in Lingan some 15 kilometres away. Apparently, he moved from one to the other as the mood, or necessity, demanded.

He had so many laudable qualities: He was a ferociously hard worker, invariably dependable in practical matters, and he was always there for a fight or showdown if necessary. He also had a phenomenal brain which was not only acute and agile, but was filled to the brim with a vast compendium of knowledge ranging from the structure of the Nazi Party, to the lives of the mayors of New York, to the history of the Communist Party, to municipal government in Hyderabad, India, to the Viennese transit system, to the grammar of a variety of foreign languages.

Indeed, his obsession with detail, especially if it were esoteric, was responsible for our not having his autobiography in our libraries. For some months I was the editor of this would-be production, but every time I took anything out --no matter how irrelevant-- he would put it right back in plus additional, even more arcane, material. Eventually, I gave up and backed out as, indeed, did the University of Cape Breton, which, having agreed to publish one large volume, became exasperated when Paul insisted that the number be expanded to three.

In such matters, as indeed in almost everything he did, MacEwan was utterly driven, as if by a demon which was lashing him onwards into ever more precarious territory. Frequently, when he had the bit between his teeth for some self-serving scheme or offensive against a real or perceived enemy, he seemed like a man possessed. At such times, rational argument was useless: One had to wait until he had calmed down, hoping that the more fantastical elements of his objective had disappeared in the interim.

For a man who was so obviously intelligent, Paul could be extraordinarily naïve or even obtuse. He seldom seemed to know what would "fly", what would be acceptable to others, or what would be practical under the circumstances. He felt that if he bulldozed on with a plan hard enough and often enough, it would automatically succeed, just as he often believed that if he wanted something to happen badly enough it would actually transpire. When reality subsequently kicked in, he would seem stupefied and shake his head with incredulity. But he never seemed to learn lessons from these experiences, and within days he would be charging at another equally unattainable windmill.

During one election, I received a phone call from Lloyd Shaw (Alexa McDonough's father), strangely asking me to meet him at the premier's office. When I got there, Lloyd was with Jerry Regan, who showed me a document one of his staff had recovered from the copying machine.

It was a letter purporting to be from Regan to Pinky Gaum, Paul's Conservative opponent in Cape Breton Nova, intimating that the Liberals were running a weak candidate in order to help Pinky defeat Paul. Shaw and Regan asked me to deal with what was an obvious forgery audaciously manufactured in the premier's own offices, presumably at the dead of night. I immediately called the worthy Bill Mozvik and asked him to root through the boxes in the back room of the campaign headquarters. Sure enough, Bill found thousands of these forgeries and was as shocked as he was nervous over the discovery. I asked him to take them all out to the city dump and burn the lot, which he dutifully did.

Paul's volatility and unpredictability gave me many restless nights and nervous mornings; there would be periods during which I was afraid to open the Cape Breton *Post* for fear it would reveal some fresh flamboyance or controversial statement. And there was no point in trying to get him to act with more circumspection, because if I did it would feed his paranoia and lead to his saying that was "in with" his enemies.

Much of Paul's obsessive behaviour had to do with money. He never had enough of it, and was always looking for ways to get his hands on more, repeatedly asking friends and colleagues for "loans" which he seldom, if ever, repaid. I did not know why he was always in such desperate need of funds, for he certainly never spent it on himself, frequently wearing worn and soiled clothes and sleeping on the floor of the caucus office. For me, that will remain the greatest of a number of unsolved mysteries surrounding this extraordinary man.

But his constituents loved him and returned him to the Legislature in nine elections and on four different "tickets"—NDP, Independent, Cape Breton Labour Party, and Liberal. He was in the Legislature for 33 successive years, an all-time record in the history of Nova Scotia.

Those interested in finding out more about the idiosyncratic Paul MacEwan should read Ian Stewart's book *Politics on the Edge: The Remarkable Career of Paul MacEwan*.

Vince MacLean

My first acquaintance with Vince MacLean was when, as a wet-behind-the-ears, newly-elected MLA, he was appointed Speaker of the House, something I considered one of Gerald Regan's worst acts. I loathed him because he was a spikey, nasty, highly-partisan Speaker, obviously trying to ingratiate himself with the Boss in order to get into the cabinet (it worked), and some of his rulings from the Chair reflected both rancour and bias.

However, over the years I greatly altered my opinion of him and came to see that, if somewhat marred by excessive partisanship and occasional flashes of spite, he was a man of knowledge, understanding and considerable ability who, had he been given the chance, would have become an outstanding premier. I also thought I could understand that the strange grimaces and semi snarls which he sometimes emitted actually stemmed from a kind of shyness, not from irascibility or malice. I came to like Vince a great deal, and it was because of him that I joined the Liberal Party in 1990. I thought he was quite badly treated by his party—despicably by many members—and I was proud to vote in his favour on the motion of confidence which he barely won at, I think, the 1992 party convention, a result which led to his stepping down from the party leadership. When he announced that he would be going, we were treated to the most disgusting kind of guttersnipe journalism from CBC's Paul Withers, who asked if Vince had been paid to quit. The CBC has reached many egregious and ignominious lows, but few as revolting as that.

Vince and I were quite friendly for some years, then drifted apart, largely because, in an email exchange, he touched my most ultra-sensitive trigger—Israel. If I get even the slightest whiff of what might be anti-Semitism, I am out the door. In any event, Vince gave good service to both the City of Sydney and Nova Scotia and I wish him and Natalie and all their children and grandchildren the very best life has to offer.

Alexa McDonough

Alexa, who died in January, 2022, was certainly a remarkable woman and politician. I do not need to repeat her many achievements here. They have been more than adequately enumerated elsewhere, frequently with hagiographic overfullness. But she was a woman, not a god: like most of us, with good and bad sides.

My association with Alexa was divided between what might be described as a period of hostility and, later, one of surprising and pleasant reconciliation.

Her father, Lloyd Shaw, introduced me to her in the early 1970s, when she was a Liberal. She subsequently joined the NDP, but I saw and heard little of her until later in the decade. During the two years prior to my resignation as party leader in 1980, she demonstrated the zeal of the convert to an extraordinary degree, indicating her view that the party was impure in its beliefs and practices, and that she represented the true gospel. She joked to me that her nickname should be "Little Polly Purebred".

I do not recall that she attacked me personally, and I never subscribed to the theory that Paul MacEwan propounded that she was at the heart of a vast, ongoing conspiracy to undermine me. That a woman with ambition would have taken advantage of a period in which I was worn out and disillusioned was only natural, so I took no special measures to limit her activity and certainly never assigned an "attack dog" to her, as Martin Kennedy suggested in his autobiography, *Always Alone.*

I was not directly involved in her political activities after I had left the party, so witnessed them only as an observer. Her methods, her tactics struck me as unusually unscrupulous and intolerant, and she surely had the "killer instinct" said to be necessary for success in politics. She shamefully exploited the fact that she was the lone woman in the Legislature, something in which neither Gladys Porter nor Melinda MacLean, who preceded her, ever indulged. With the help of a sympathetic media she cultivated an image of Poor Little Alexa Being Bullied by the Nasty Men, when she was both tough and ruthless enough to handle the whole lot of them put together. In debate, there was never any give and take. If an opponent conceded a point, she would use it against him: she was all take and no give.

Therefore, after she had left political life and I had formed XM-LAS (the Association of former Members of the Nova Scotia Legislature) in 2013, I expected her to give me a rough ride. I could not have been more wrong. Not only was she respectful of the Presidency, but gave me unstinting support in disputes between the Chair and other members. And she scrupulously adhered to the rule that nothing in our conduct or affairs be partisan in nature. In a nutshell, she was an exceedingly pleasant and cooperative colleague with whom I could work harmoniously and enjoy many cordial conversations.

That is how I choose to remember her.

Stephen McNeil

Elsewhere in this book, I have said that I think Stephen McNeil is one of the best premiers in Nova Scotia history, an assertion I happily repeat here. In an era when politicians and public alike seem to believe that ever more spending and borrowing are signs of virtue, goodness and light, McNeil kept as firm a hand on the fiscal tiller as was practicable (much more than the Opposition Conservatives would have done), and for that alone he deserves high praise and gratitude. And, apart from a few lapses, I think his judgment was sound.

His overall sober and serious demeanour kept a cap on extravagant adventures which cabinet members doubtless wanted to pursue at breakneck speed, and that allowed the voters to feel safe and reassured that the helm of the ship of state was in good hands. In that respect, I always felt that Stephen was the natural inheritor of Robert Stanfield, whose halting, hesitant, thoughtful manner of expression was (contrary to Opposition wishful thinking) an enormous plus with the voters. Nova Scotians may be temporarily impressed by glamour, pizzazz and fireworks, but when push comes to shove, they prefer a leader who shows humility and steadiness, rather than one who is a "big feeling" Mr. Know-it-all.

But I think it was because he felt it incumbent and fitting that Stephen conducted himself with caution and modesty, not because he was incapable, for example, of great oratory: Anyone who heard his address at John Buchanan's memorial service would have to admit it was one of the finest, most uplifting and beautifully delivered speeches ever heard in Nova Scotia. I whispered to my wife, "If he did a tour and spoke like that at every stop, he would sweep the province in the next election."

In addition, on a one-to-one basis, Stephen is a charming and exceedingly likeable man with whom it is always a pleasure to chat; unlike many politicians, he does not look over your shoulder to see if there is anyone more important coming along!

There were two occasions on which he disappointed me. The first was when, gratuitously I thought, he opined that the statue of General Edward Cornwallis (the founder of Halifax) should be removed because an unknown, unelected, unrepresentative extremist ranted and raved that the statue was (what else?) "racist". I would have expected someone of Stephen's knowledge and common sense to have calmly pointed out that humans erect statues to statesmen, soldiers, et al, because they are seminal or integral to our development as a civilization, not because we necessarily agree with everything they did and said back in the mists of time.

The other occasion was when, I believe, he allowed Finance Minister Diana Whalen to back him into a corner over the Film Tax Credit, a tool which had brought tens of millions of dollars in productions to our province, employing thousands of people. Ever since the tax credit really got going, when I was Manager of the fund under David Nantes, bureaucrats at the Department of Finance had been trying to kill it, because in its form as a rebate it appeared on the books as a public expenditure. With every new minister these bureaucrats went to work with fresh hope and renewed vigour and, I believe, that where they had failed with previous rookie ministers they succeeded with Diana by misrepresenting the facts, especially relative to liabilities and benefits. She then announced the program's evisceration at a Board of Trade meeting and the government and premier were stuck with it. It was a sad day which cost the province a great industry and drove hundreds of skilled people away to other provinces. [In the interest of full disclosure, I must record that it also cost me about a third of my income.]

Just after the 2021 Nova Scotia election, in which the Liberals were thrashed, I told Stephen that, had he continued to lead the party, he would have won a third term; not a big win, but with a small majority. I still think that, and I for one would have been happy to have had this exceptional man lead us for another four years.

François Mitterand

[In the mid-1960s, when he was 50 years old, Mitterrand began a long affair with Anne Pingeot, a 30-year-old campaign volunteer. In 1974, she gave birth to their daughter, Mazarine. The Secret Service was ordered to keep this secret and it did not become public until 1994.]

The most arrogant man I ever met was François Mitterand, who was president of the French Republic from 1981 to 1995. When we were introduced he looked down his nose at me as if I was dung on his shoe, and when I tried to converse in my admittedly rusty French, he made a face of disgust and flounced away. When he chaired sessions of the conference which we were attending, he acted in an autocratic manner, choosing simply not to see any delegates whose views he did not expect to like.

One night, Mitterand was holding forth with great passion about the need for better funded public schools, declaring that they were the cornerstone of a socialist society. One of his senior aides was sitting with me at the back of the room and I commented that, while I did not much care for his boss's manner, I was impressed by his sincerity.

"Bullshit," the man said. "Both kinds of his kids are at private schools."

"Really?" I was surprised. "What do you mean 'both kinds of kids'?"

"Danielle's three boys and the bastard," he replied.

Peter Nicholson

Of all the politicians I met during my lifetime, Peter Nicholson was by far the most decent, honourable and trustworthy. If that were not sufficient in any human being, Peter was also highly intelligent, immensely able, and extraordinarily competent. He was a first-class Minister of Finance and, if I am not mistaken, not only left the budget balanced when the Tories took over in 1978, but also left a more than manageable provincial debt. In addition, he was an able speaker and debater, and was great company.

I was very sad when he lost his seat to Greg Kerr (although Greg also a very decent guy) in Annapolis West. In light of the universal esteem in which Peter was held, I was moved to suggest to incoming premier Buchanan that he break with precedent and appoint Peter Speaker of the House, since it would not take much of an amendment to the House of Assembly Act to allow a Speaker who was not an MLA. But John worried that it would upset the party and, in any event, said he wanted to reward the incoming MLA for Hants West, Ron Russell.

Gerald Regan

The world is pretty much divided into those who knew, and therefore liked, Gerald Regan, and those who did not know him, and therefore did not. The latter are everywhere to be found, chiefly because, they will swear to you, that they know he was guilty of any number of egregious sins and crimes, most notably those of which he was completely acquitted (rape, attempted rape, indecent assault and forcible confinement) by a majority female jury in 1998. This syndrome was typified by an exchange I had with a supposedly intelligent, professional medical man, who asserted that, regardless of the court decision, Regan was "definitely guilty". When I asked him to explain himself, he first said he had it on "unimpeachable authority". When I pursued this, he eventually said it came from a friend of his daughter's whom he believed was "trustworthy".

A more concrete example of the way innuendo, gossip, suspicion and personal or political animus were revealed when subjected to scrutiny, was when my secretary told me, quite unequivocally, that her own sister had been raped by Gerald Regan. This was repeated, almost traded on, for years until, eventually, the sister related on a CBC television program that Regan had visited her in his capacity as her MLA to respond to her request for assistance. While he was there, she told the interviewer, she felt very uneasy. No advance was made, no physical contact established, only that she had felt uncomfortable. From this thinnest of gruel, she and her sister dined out for years on a false accusation of full-blooded rape.

When their unsupported accusations are revealed to have no basis other than gossip or hearsay, the Regan haters resort to the nonsensical fiction that Regan's lawyer, Edward Greenspan, had mercilessly bullied and browbeaten his accusers on the witness stand until they were in tears and would say anything to make the alleged persecution stop. That version of events serves only to prove that these people were never in the court. I was there, and nothing even remotely like that occurred. Greenspan never even raised his voice and, patiently, almost kindly, took accusers through their evidence; evidence on which they were extraordinarily confused, contradicting themselves to the point where their credibility was in tatters. It seemed clear to me that these poor wo-men had been put up to this sad misadventure (again, I suspected, though could not prove, the sinister hand of Donald Ripley) and that their motives were so confused and murky that not even they fully understood why they were there.

One evening, in the premier's office after the Legislature had risen and a group of us were sitting around drinking Scotch, col-ourful reporter Doug Harkness said to the premier, "Listen Preem, you couldn't get laid in a whorehouse even if you had ten credit cards and a thousand dollar bill".

Based upon my extensive experience with Regan at home and abroad, I would say Harkness was not far off the mark.

Over the decades I was with Jerry Regan in a variety of places, settings and company, and not once did I see him behave inappro-priately with a woman, even though opportunities were clearly available. And when it might seem that women were more than willing, it was Jerry, not they, who brought the encounters to a close.

One example must suffice. On the occasion on which we went to London to host the previously-mentioned banquet for Princess Anne, the following evening we all went out to dinner. At an adja-cent table were two young American women, only one of whose names I can now remember: Ann Lindsay. On learning that we were staying at the fabled Savoy Hotel, they expressed a wish to come back with us and take a look at it.

We went to Jerry's suite, then after a while the other woman and I went out to get some refreshment, which we took up to my room. There we nattered away until about an hour later the phone rang. It was Ann calling so I listened in.

"For Christ's sake," she said, "come and rescue me. I'm bored to tears. He just showed me photographs of his wife and kids for the fourth time."

So, the next time anyone tells you they know, ask for their proof —actual proof, not supposition, gossip, hearsay or malicious lies.

Overall, I found Regan to be highly intelligent, well-read, sharp, alert and wonderful company because he had a devilish sense of humour. I think he was a competent and able premier, especially fiscally, who, had it not been for the timing of the energy crisis, would likely have received a third term in office. It has been my pleasure and privilege to have been friends with Jerry Regan and all his family for more than half a century.

Tom Selleck

Most actors, including big name movie stars, are not thinkers, analyzers or rationalists; they are all about emotions, snap judgments, virtue signalling, and following whatever "line" has been handed down from on high. In their off-screen lives, they attempt to reproduce the "rush" they feel when emoting before the camera and successfully delivering lines written for them by others. Since being logical, objective and balanced is unlikely to produce that kind of feeling of moral superiority, most adopt a quasi-leftist, sanctimonious, judgmental posture, requiring them to slobber over approved "woke" or politically-correct people and positions, and righteously condemn those whom they have been instructed are "right wing", "racist", "sexist", "homophobic", "Islamophobic" etc. etc.

Tom Selleck is the diametrical opposite of these kinds of actors. He is not only a consummate professional, precise and punctilious, but is also a thinker who is widely read and possessed of considerable powers of understanding. This is why, sadly, he is an exception, if not an outcast, in the Hollywood fraternity, most members of which are knee-jerk lemmings.

Also, for a man of his many accomplishments, Tom is not vain or boastful, nor is he clamorous for the plaudits of the crowd other than a desire to produce a top quality product. Unlike his friend, Sam Elliott (another most likeable man) who will leave the set to go out into the street and mix with fans, Tom is concentrated on work, so keeps himself to himself and the few with whom he is shooting the scene. The world outside belongs outside.

It has been a great pleasure and privilege to have known Tom, and to have worked with him on something like seven productions over a ten-year period.

Roland Thornhill

Rollie Thornhill is one of my favourite people. He is highly intelligent, wise, informed, well-read, amusing, and among the best company to be found anywhere. He was an extremely able minister, likely the best political minister John Buchanan ever had, and was a euphonic and resonant speaker whom it was always a pleasure to hear. When I first got to know him, I was (as I have said in a previous chapter) extremely naïve in political matters and remained so for some years, but, by contrast, Rollie was artful and circumspect, displaying a far greater understanding of people than I.

Rollie was a Member of the Legislature for just shy of 20 years, and had it not been for some bad luck he would have become premier. When he was running for the leadership of the Conservative Party, old information about his private dealings with banks (he made a deal which anyone in their right mind would also have accepted) were deliberately recirculated, with the result that he lost out to Donald Cameron, he of page girl and entrapment fame related in a previous chapter.

In this connection, I might mention something which few living, and certainly not Rollie, have hitherto known. On two occasions I turned up to the office to be told that mysterious packages had been slipped under the door. Each contained details of Rollie's financial transactions considerably before they became public. Both caucus members and the staff clamoured for me to use the information in the House, but I refused and tore the papers into shreds.

Had he been successful in obtaining the party leadership, I am convinced Rollie would have been an attractive, outstanding, and level-headed premier who would have been able to gain the government a further term.

19: At the crossroads

"Give every other human being every right
you claim for yourself."—Robert G. Ingersoll

It has become a well-worn cliché that older people look back through rose-tinted glasses and tell the young that "things were better in my day."

On a personal level, I am happier and healthier than at any other time in my life, largely as a result of my marrying Caroll Anne in 2018. But I am convinced that, at least in one area with which my life has been preoccupied, politics, things *were* better when I was young.

There, the situation is worse because the freedoms which are central to the survival of a Judaeo-Christian small "l" liberal civilization are on the chopping block. Daily, they are being assaulted by those who are masquerading as "progressives". They not only tell us what we can and cannot say, but also what we should think. Those who dissent from the approved mainstream line are excoriated, persecuted and punished. Dissenters are "de-platformed", lose their jobs, are subjected to judicial harassment and are slapped with any number of denigratory labels. And, in lock-step with governments, social media giants are daily exercising censorship on opinions they regard as deviating from the accepted norm.

An example of this is that this book was originally commissioned by a publisher at the urging of a third party, but when it was finished they both rejected it in an extraordinarily illogical and hysterical manner. It praised the wrong idols and criticized sacred cows. They wanted me to tell my story the way *they* would have told it, replacing my biases with their own.

When I was an MLA, one could pretty much say anything one wanted. For example, one could even talk about race and immigration.

Logic should tell us that every citizen of Canada, whether they be brand new or "old stock", has a right to hold and express an opinion on immigration. Back then, it would have been legitimate to discuss the rate of immigration, how many would be self-sufficient as opposed to becoming charges upon the state, how many might have views antithetical to democracy and gender equality, and whether the incomers might contain any terrorists.

Today, an MLA could say none of this without unleashing a maelstrom of hysterical invective, screams of "racism", "white supremacy", motions of censure and excoriation in the media.

If we are truly to have a free society, then we should welcome not only a diversity of people, but of opinion, too. That is the measure of an adult civilization.

Jeremy Akerman

20: Roll of Honour

Those listed here, both living and dead, were seminal in my development, crucially important to my life and career, or at some point showed me kindness which I wish to acknowledge. Sadly, it is inevitable that some names will have slipped my mind, even though I can still see all their faces. If you feel you belong on this list and I have omitted you, I offer my sincere apologies.

A
Abbas, Jay
Abbas, John
Abbott, Caroline and Carl
Acland, Ann
Adams, Blaine
Adams, Rhonda
Akerman, Albert
Akerman, Alex
Akerman, Andrew
Akerman, Bernard and Audrey
Akerman, Brian
Akerman, Caroll Anne Boone-
Akerman, Ginny
Akerman Janet
Akerman, Keith
Akerman, Maurice
Akerman, Michael and Pat
Akerman, Michael and Sue

Akerman, Zanna
Alcock, Leslie and Elizabeth
Anderson, Frances
Anderson, Gillian
Andrea, Glenn
Armitage, Brad
Armitage, Jack
Arnold, Doug
Arthur, Karen
Ashworth, Dennis and Diane

B
Babin, Joyce
Bacon, Roger
Baker, Kathy
Barrett, Denise
Bateman, David
Bates, Ages and Emmett
Bauchman, Laurel

Baydon, Linda
Baxter, Charles
Beare, John and Jean
Bellefontaine, Lori
Belmore, Betty
Bentley, David
Bennett, Glenda
Bennett, Nigel
Bernsen, Corbyn
Best, Whitfield
Bolivar, Randy
Bibby, Ian
Bickerton, Carmen
Bigelow, Kathryn
Bockstael, Robert
Bond, Mary
Boone, Frank and Ann
Boone, Gerald and Shirley
Boone, Shelly
Boone, Weldon
Brandon, Michael
Brandon, Steven
Brewster, Raymond
Brewster, Sandy and Dolena
Briffett, Bethana
Brison, Scott
Brown, Bill
Brown, Garnet and Betty
Brown, Guy
Brown, John Rod and Aileen
Brown, Sheldon
Bryanton, Brenda
Bryson, Peter and Patricia
Boutilier, Fabian
Bowen, Clive

Buchanan, John and Mavis

C
Cable, Paulette
Cabrita, Harry
Cabrita, Suzanna
Campbell, Freddie
Cameron, Bob
Cameron, Hugh and Ann
Cameron, R.B
Cameron, R.B. Jr.
Candow, Bhreagh
Candow, Liam
Candy, Rob and Theresa
Card, Heather
Carrigan, Owen
Cazes, Henri
Cazes, Jean-Michel
Chaisson, Valerie
Chernin, Isaac
Choyce, Leslie
Christie, Peter and Joan
Clarke, Al and Hazel
Clarke, Joe and Diane
Clarke, Steve and Hazel
Clease, George and Doreen
Clease, Adrian
Close, Nicole
Cochran, Andrew
Cochran, Maxine
Cochrane, John
Cook, Melinda
Cooper, George
Coish, Diane
Colpitts, Mark

Columbus, Jack
Corbett, John "Bunny"
Corbett, Frank "Nanky"
Corston, Hugh
Cosman, Francene
Craig, Jack and Joan
Crossley, David and Elizabeth
Currie, Keith

D
Dalton, Diana
David, Jim
Davidson, Andrea
Davidson, Katherine
Davis-Brennan, Nora
Dean, John and Shirley
Dechman, Marie
Defrieze, John Roddy
Devlin, Paul
Deveau, Alan
DeWolf, Terry
Diab, Lena
Diab, Maroun
Dial, Adam
Dial, Gail and Roger
Dial, Marshall
Dobson, Carol
Donat, Richard and Maggie
Donahoe, Arthur and Carolyn
Donahoe, Terrance R.B.
Donovan, Phil
Downe, Don
Doucet, George and Ginny
Douglas, Tommy and Irma
Doucet, Michelle
Doucet, Vida

Dumaresq, Sid and Sandy
Dunsworth, John
Dunsworth, Sarah
Dunton, John and Hope

E
Eagles, Bill
Eagles, Gordon and Belle
Elliott, Shirley

F
Faulkener, Wayne
Filiatraut, Derek
Fisher, Ron
Fiske, Ralph
Fitzgerald, Kenny
Fitzgerald, Thom
Flemming, Harry
Fleming, Bill
Floyd, Bob Rev.
Foot, Michael
Foulkes, George Lord
Ford, Harrison
Fraser, Darcy
Fraser, Joan
Fraser, Kathryn
Fraser, Roddie
Fudge, Nathan
Fulton, Gerry
Furzee, Richard

G
Gallivan, Noel
Gardere, Jean Paul
Gardner Jesse J.
Gaudin, Rosemary

Gervais, Charlotte
Grant, Rachel
Gibbons, Carole
Gilbert, Rosemary
Gillies, Jim
Goodfellow, Walter
Gordon, Sandy
Graham, Danny
Graham, Glenn
Green, Sidney and Shalima
Grant, Adam

H
Hagen, Elizabeth
Hagen, Joanne
Hadley, Richard
Haley, Jack and Annette
Halman, Valerie
Hambling, Ivor
Hamilton, Linda
Harding, Aubrey
Hargitay, Mariska
Harmon, Robert
Harrison, Walter
Harte, James and Jean
Harte, Ian
Harwood, Penelope
Hatfield, Richard
Hatt, Shauna
Hawkins, Jack and Mona
Helppi Jari-Matti
Hendsbee, David
Hennen, Albert
Hiscocks, Heather
Holcomb, Rod

Holland, Bruce and Fe
Horner, Clyde
How, Harry and Juanita
Hubley, Mark
Huk, John and Wanda
Huston, John

J
Jarrett, Nancy
Jackman, Jerry
Jebailey Rania
Jemmett, David
Jollotta, Barbi
Jollotta, Liona
Jonatanson, Debi
Joudrey, JJ
Jones, Gareth
Jones, Joan

K
Kavanagh, Frank
Kelly, Bill and Helena
Kemsley, John and Margaret
Kennedy, Laura Lee and Nathan
Kennedy, Martin
Kettless, Ray
Kimber, Jeannie
King, David and Gillian
King, Leonard and Myrtle
King, Mary
Kinley, Jim
Knight, Barbara
Knight, Bob and Kay
Knight, Bryan

Maclean, Vince and Natalie
MacLeod, Donald Allistair
MacGuire, Frank
MacDonald, Adele
MacDonald, Angus F.
MacDonald, Blaise and Lois
MacLeod, Geri Lynne
MacLeod, Mike
MacLeod, Moira
MacLellan, Russell
MacPherson, David and Dayle
MacPherson, Marnie
MacPherson, Will and Margie
Madden, John
Mahoney, Mike
Marchbank, Allan
Marchand, Narcisse
Marriott, Norma
Marginson, Karen
Markle, Peter
Marsh, Bill and Sadie
Mattocks, Fred
Mattocks, Michael
Matheson, Harold
Matheson, Joe and Mary
Matheson, Murdock and Ida
Matheson, Reeves
McAulay, Ernie
McConnell, Richard and
   Stephanie
McDonald, Bill
McDougall, Michael
McGrath, Ruth
McGrath, Shelagh
McInnis, Eddie

McInnis, Frank and Joan
McInnis, Tom
McIsaac, John
McNeil, Shirley
McNeil, Stephen
McNeil, Kenzie
McNutt Laura
McNutt, Scott
Meekison, Peter
Meloni, Rodolfo
Mendelson, Gerry
Merchie, Todd
Mian, Maqbul and Cowsa
Mikardo, Ian
Mio, Gene and Roxanna
Millington, Carol
Milsom, Geoff
Mitchell, Donald and Rachel
Mitchell, George
Mitchell, Kevin
Mozvik, Bill
Muise, Mickey and Eileen
Munce, Dave
Murphy, Evelyn
Murphy, Erin
Murphy, Kevin
Murphy, Wrin
Murray, Emlyn
Murray, Peter and Rosie
Musial, Charlie

N
Nantes, David
Natal, Dennis
Neal, Peter

S
Savage, John and Margaret
Savage, Michael
Schreyer, Ed and Lily
Schwartz, Irving
Scwartz, Marty
Scott, Sandra
Scott Savage, Alexina
Scotton, Cliff
Selleck, Tom
Semple, Will
Sergejewski, Sasha
Sheehy, Gerry
Shoveller, Joan
Simms, Joyce
Shurko, Jason
Shurko, John
Shurko, Charlotte
Skinner, Carl
Skinner, Bill and Allie
Smith, Arthur and Gladys
Smith, Earl and Marion
Smith, Gordon and Annie Mae
Smith, Ike
Smith, Maurice and Jane
Smith, Rob
Smith, Jo-Ann
Smith, Mike
Snow, George and Marjorie
Solowij, Adam
Solowij, Cynthia
Solowij, Trudi
Spacek, Sissy
Sparks, Jeremiah
Stalker, Bob

Stamp, Joanne
Steele, Frazer and Pat
Steele, Graham
Steinfeld, Mark and Esther
Stirling, Laird and Carolyn
Stone, Lloyd and Jessie
Strange, Jane
Strong, Peter and Frances
Sullivan, Alan and Stephanie
Sullivan, Allan E.
Sutton, Austin and Marsha
Sweeney, Jim
Sweeney, Tom
Swift, Amy

T
Taylor, Lorne
Timmons, Jeremy
Thomas, Joe
Thompson, David
Thompson, Hugh
Thornhill, Roland and Bonnie
Till, Eric
Timmons, Jeremy
Toole, Barry and Janet
Townsend, Trish
Tremblay, JP
Thorne, Chaz
Turnbull, Eddie

V
Veniot, Harvey
Verbeski, Bernie
Viera, Harry
Vogel, Joe and Jeannie

Vollick, Cooper

W
Wadden, Ursula
Wade, Angela
Wakefield, Susan
Wallace, Ron
Waters, Russell
Watkins, Lyndon
Waybrett, Dewy
Weldon, Dick and Joan
Wellington, David
Wells, Ricky
Werner, Peter
Wetmore, Andrew
Wheaton, Jeff
White, Clare
Whitley, Raymond and Judy
Wilcox, Richard
Wilkinson, David and Ina
Williams, Leighton
Williams, Mary
Wilton, Terry and Josie
Wolk, Andy
Worthen, Jim
Wood, Sean and Jody
Wright, Gordon

Y
Yaffee, Barbara
Yakimchuk, Dan and Ina
Yemini, Shaula
Yetman, Gerald
Young, Brian
Young, Brian J
Young, Dolores

Young, John and Carol

Z
Zann, Lenore
Zinck, Maurice
Zwicker, Bruce

Jeremy Akerman

21: Filmography

At the time of assembling this book in 2022, I have taken part in 143 "shoots", and have played 135 leading, supporting, or principal roles.

Feature films

Year	Show	Character	Director
2017	The Healer	Father Lindsay	Paco Arango
2013	Blackbird	Don Kirby	Jason Buxton
2012	Cloudburst	Justice	Thom Fitzgerald
2011	Hobo with a Shotgun	Chief Wakeum	Jason Eisner
2010	Amelia	Sergeant	Mira Nair
2008	Just Buried	Rollie	Chaz Thorne
2007	Poor Boy's Game	Mello	Clement Virgo
2006	Trailer Park Boys	Judge Smith	Mike Clattenburg
2005	Hole In One	Robert Watson	Richard Leeds
2004	K-19 The Widowmaker	Captain Tsvetskov	Kathryn Bigelow
2004	Virginia's Run	Huntington Crane	Peter Markle
2004	Julie Walking Home	Samuel	Agnieska Holland

Television movies

Year	Title	Character	Director
2014	Lizzie Borden	Judge Blaidsell	Nick Gomez
2013	Titanic: The Aftermath	Harold Wingate	Marion Milne
2012	Jesse Stone: Benefit of the Doubt	Carter Hansen	Dick Lowry
2011	November Christmas	Rev. Bob Danforth	Robert Harmon
2011	Jesse Stone: Innocents Lost	Carter Hansen	Dick Lowry
2011	Jesse Stone: No Remorse	Carter Hansen	Robert Harmon
2010	Darwin's Darkest Hour	Parslow	John Bradshaw
2009	Jesse Stone: Thin Ice	Carter Hansen	Robert Harmon
2008	The Memory Keeper's Daughter	The Minister	Mick Jackson
2008	The Circuit	Charlie	Peter Werner
2007	Jesse Stone: Sea Change	Carter Hansen	Robert Harmon
2007	Shades of Black	Bud McDougald	Alex Chappelle
2006	Christmas Wedding	Oxbow	Michael Zinberg
2006	Codebreakers	General Douglas MacArthur	Rod Holcomb
2005	Dive from Clausen's Pier	Morton Fraser	Harry Winer
2005	Jesse Stone: Stone Cold	Carter Hansen	Robert Harmon
2005	The Plain Truth	Judge Herbert Jones	Paul Shapiro
2005	The River Man	Lt. Don Downing	Bill Eagles
2005	Sleep Murders	Edward	Andrew Currie
2004	Finding John Christmas	Antonovich	Andy Wolk

Year	Title	Character	Director
2004	Martha Inc.	Weilding	Jason Ensler
2003	Rush of Fear	Farmer Brown	Walter Klenhard
2003	Too Young to Be a Dad	Family Attorney	Ava Gardos
2003	Gracie's Choice	Judge Irwin Donner	Peter Werner
2002	The Christmas Shoes	Tom Wilson	Andy Wolk
2002	Passion and Prejudice	Deputy Banks	Karen Arthur
2002	Town Without Christmas	Sheriff Bridges	Andy Wolk
2002	Glimpse of Hell	Senator John Warner	Mikhail Saloman
2002	Songs in Ordinary Time	Monsignor Cushing	Rod Holcomb

TV series and mini-series

Year	Title	Character bold = series regular italics = principal	Director
2020	Chapelwaite	Christopher Morgan	Various
2019	Trailer Park Boys	Judge Tickleberry	Various
2019	Mr. Dee	Minister of Education	Various
2019	Forgive Me, season III	**Father Gene**	Thom Fitzgerald
2017	Trailer Park Boys, season X	Judge Tickleberry	Various
2016	Sex and Violence, season III	**Seamus MacDonald**	Various

Year	Title	Character bold = series regular italics = principal	Director
2015	Forgive Me, season II	**Father Gene**	Thom Fitzgerald
2015	Sex and Violence, season II	**Seamus MacDonald**	Thom Fitzgerald
2014	The Book of Negroes	*Field Surgeon*	Clement Virgo
2013	Sex and Violence	**Seamus MacDonald**	Thom Fitzgerald
2013	Forgive Me	**Father Gene**	Thom Fitzgerald
2012	The Drunk and On Drugs Happy Funtime Hour	*Dr. Fieldivory*	Ron Murphy
2006	October Crisis	The Coroner	Don MacBrearty
2005	Trudeau II	Gordon Robertson	Tim Southam
2005	Snakes and Ladders	**Charles Lamar**	Sterla Gunnarson
2004	Shattered City	Rev. George Adams	Bruce Pitman
2003	Trudeau	Minister Bellman	Gerry Ciccoritti
2003	Trailer Park Boys	Crown Prosecutor	Mike Clattenburg
2000-2001	Pit Pony	**Everett Frawley**	Various

Shorts

Year	Title	Character bold = lead	Director
2013	Flush	**Howard Castle**	Megan Wennberg
2013	Goodbye Robot Army	**Maximilian Brand**	Greg Jackson
2011	Bernard the Magician	Frank	Megan Wennberg
2009	Home Invasion	Henry Warehelm	David Stewart
2008	Prism	Rabbi Mendi	Evan Eisanstaadt

The author and the late John Dunsworth on the set of "Forgive Me"

Jeremy Akerman

About the author

Jeremy Akerman is an adoptive Nova Scotian who has lived in the province for 58 years (as of 2022). In that time he has been an archaeologist, a radio announcer, a politician, a senior civil servant, a newspaper editor and a film actor.

He is painter of landscapes and portraits, a singer of Irish folk songs, a lover of wine, and a devotee of history, especially of the British Labour Party.